Old Mans Rants

Tony Snow

 pencil

ISBN 978-93-5458-800-6
© Tony Snow 2021
Published in India 2021 by Pencil

A brand of
One Point Six Technologies Pvt. Ltd.
123, Building J2, Shram Seva Premises,
Wadala Truck Terminal, Wadala (E)
Mumbai 400037, Maharashtra, INDIA
E connect@thepencilapp.com
W www.thepencilapp.com

Author biography

I'll begin with why I am writing this book it started a long time ago when I had been judged for things that were not my fault and from that moment my life snowballed twisted and turned to where I am today, that was a long winding road to get to this point some of this book will flow and you will get it other parts no doubt will go off the charts to a new demotion making a lot of sense in this crazy ass world that we live in, it will move here moving there and maybe back.

I start my rant with something that should be close to everyone's heart so go read chapter 1 now.

CONTENTS

Chapter 1 Child Abuse

Mental, physical or sexual abuse, it is not right on any level for any reason, no matter if you're in a bad mood or you get off on hurting a child.

Physically abused and mentally I have been not sexual, thank fuck. Beatings at the hands of my Mother and stepfather were brutal.

Mother would always say, "I'm going to hit you so fucking hard you won't be able to sit down for a week" or I am going to hit you so fucking hard ill make your ass bleed"

What she said is what you got black and blue and yes, you could not sit for a week either and it was hard to sleep. Step-Father occasionally picked me up by my ears, hit my head into walls in my bedroom, which were always fun, right? No, I think not.

Other times with his fists or whatever was close to him, my Mother loved to play games mental games ones that would break your spirit and the outside world would say I wonder why he never went to his own Mother's funeral I fucking wonder.

People are judgemental of things they do not know the truth of, but that's ok. I don't mind people frowning looking at me for just being me judged for being different.

All because my Mother killed my step farther by knifing him in the chest. No one wanted anything to do with the kid that had just gone through hell and back. No one wanted to lend a hand, no one wanted to even say hello or even smile.

It's not like no one knew me personally. I still remember their faces and how they turned their heads in shame. For me, stunned at first, I scrambled to understand the gravity of violence.

Most likely, writing this book, people will talk and say, how could Tony say such things as child abuse? Or my time in hell? But that's ok! Fuck you,

Like, the housemate that I lived with all those years ago, she loved to fight, loved to argue, loved to throw things at me and the mind games were on the same level as my mother always to catch you out on a lie.

I put it down to so form of control that she had an issue with, she always had to be right even when you caught her out in a lie she always had an answer and if you wanted to prove you were right, it was never worth the huge fight that was coming,

I found that people just don't want to get involved they did not want to have the stigma of jumping in on something they don't know about, but in saying, all of this I somehow made it through even though I fell through the cracks and the system failed me more than once and that's ok I'm one of the lucky ones to come through it, I almost didn't make it though I came so close to death many times,

People who hurt children parent or parents either mother or father or both no matter if it is a step parent one or both no matter if it is an uncle or an aunty or even your grandparents or not even a family member no matter if it is by hitting them with an object or your hands or mentally abuse or even worse sexually assault against a child is unforgivable!

With the churches not naming any of them by names but just to say you use your power of authority all in the name of God well it looks like you're not getting into heaven or maybe you know that there is no God that makes sense to me, No matter the reason there is no reason to hurt a child no reason at all, I believe the pope should show his hands and say enough is enough and finally name and shame them all so the families can get justice,

If you hurt a child, I hope you get everything that comes your way like a long jail term or even better let the parents pick the punishment no matter how unhuman it is as those people have taken a child's innocence away from them and most likely giving the child a complex or disorder against men or the church or even god,

No one may hurt these children, not me not you not your parent's not a Priest not even a policeman not anyone so hands off the children's truly I don't get how seeing a child naked can make you a roused?

You are just a vile human being? Or is it you are weak-minded fool who needs to hurt children to make yourself feel better, so it has truly cared for you. You sick fuck.

So you feel powerful? Watch them scream for help? Scream to be set free? Scream in pain? Does it make you feel all man? All I can really say to someone that is causing abuse go take yourself out of the picture entirely don't hurt them.,

Don't get me started with you where sexually abused by someone and now you do it to that is no excuse for what so ever as there is no excuse for that sort of behavior with a child, You hurt children because they are weaker than you and can't fight back why do you think you don't take on someone else like a man?

I'll tell you why Mr. it's because she will kick your ass and leave you bleeding and your ego could not handle that but you like children because even if they fight back you will not get hurt and you can make yourself a lot of man just by taking a child's innocence,

Why don't you just man up and take a bullet to the head and do the entire world a favor? For people that think that discipline comes only in one form and that's hurting the child as much as you can in one go like I have a good idea let's see if this type of discipline works out for the parents now you have to make sure that a child can remember said punishment otherwise no point right?

Four easy steps now step 1 cut off a piece of say your house hold garden hose the nylon type you know the old green ones that most houses had in the 80,s let's say a foot long and let's also say no matter what the child has done,

This is step 2. Make them drop their pants, not just their jeans plus undies drop them to the ground and if you see them shaking in fear, that's ok therefore we do it more so,

Now step 3 this step is very important to get this step absolutely perfect, make sure you lift your hand has high as you can and make sure that you use all your might and hit that child across the arse maybe legs and lower back if you feel like it as it does not matter don't be shy and with your other hand hold their head now trust me the child will thank you when they grow up as punishment it is the only way,

step 4 send them to their room crying and in clear pain but that's ok because people that child has now learnt a valuable lesson today and no doubt will carry all of their days, now don't you feel a lot belter I know after that type of punishment I know I do,

I am like wait up a minute I'm not down with this shit and not just because it happened to me I'm not down with it because it is child abuse it's not right on any level and if reading this and you did not cringe at all then something is wrong with you, a child is not born into this world to be abused by you even if you are the parent or a man of God or anyone in a trusted position or just anyone, truly who the fuck do you think you are?

This whole system needs a good shakeup, I see good homes were good people can't get even on the list to adopt children while you have others I know have their children around hard drugs and the system really does nothing I know this firsthand as it makes complete sense doesn't it?

Tell me if I'm wrong to leave a child in that type of place? Around drugs and real hardcore junkies all this type of child-raising is abuse and most likely these children will grow up to be a burden on society, To me, this system is fucking broken and the only people that are hurt here are the children but who cares right? Not welfare, not Government and surely not the parents themselves,

I am one of the lucky ones to come out the other side of a poor upbringing from poor food, abused mentally floggings to mum going to jail then being around people who took hard drugs and I said no to them but don't think about me think about the children that are still stuck in the type of family upbringing,

If you see something, please don't think that someone else will come along. Just man up and speak up. Let us help put a stop to all forms of child. Abuse, here is one fine example.

I've seen young children say the age of two in nappies standing on the edge of the cutter on a busy road now I pull over and pick up this child and I go knock on the door of the closest house now this bit you will get a laugh out of I know I did? Not really, as the lady opens the door, she sees me standing there with a young child in my arms she had a horrible look on her face like I was a pedophile or something she snatches the child out of my arms and screams out at her other children who are like 5 and 6 and she says you supposed to be looking after him you stupid dumb cunt boom she slams the door in my face I am like what the actual fuck I could have run over your child lady and you did not even say thank you,

Let's say for argument's sake it was me and I hit that child in my car because I did not see him at first the child would have died, and she would blame me, and I could not live with myself but somehow I was the weirdo for saving her child?

So, you can only imagine what sort of life that child is living, so what are you going to do the next time you see someone doing the wrong thing to a child? Stand up stand tall and make the call don't be a pussy because you don't want to get involved please people do it for the children, How is this normal to abuse a child mentally or sexually does it make you feel all-powerful and all that shit do you really like getting inside the child's mind playing within it like a football saying things to make them feel good then strip them down like they are not even human?

All I know about this is if you can't either control your mouth or control your temper than don't have children and don't get with someone who has children I know what it is like to be at the hands of violence, You know it is not normal right? sexual abuse, emotional abuse, physical abuse,

I mean, come on, we are all human, right? So, it's ok is it when you leave brushing? How do you feel when you know they grow up one day? It might turn them into ladies of the night or just junkies or even abusers themselves? But still your need to defile a child all for your own selfish needs,

I know a few people that have seen abused, and it happens more than we release they say that it's always someone close to you like your father, mother's brother or uncle, for me, I never suffered being sexually abused but mentally abused and physically abused but not sexually,

This has been going on since humans lived in caves, but this is not an excuse anymore just because you want to act like a Neanderthal? Or am I living in some type of pipe dream? There is an old saying do unto others that you would want to be done to yourself, so fair is fair it not. Even an eye for an eye or tooth for a tooth?

What man thought flocking into his stepson was a great idea when he was the adult and I was the child he also seemed to love hitting my mother as well as me and after witnessing what ended up being my fate or just destiny came looking for me and it's not like my mother was a saint and I'm not giving my step farther the green light but she was also abusive,

Now you can't be like that with a guy he is just a brute old school army dude and I know if you had to sleep with him it was not out of love or being in love I know he forced you more than once what he or both of you guys failed to understand I could hear and it's not just what I heard I seen on over,

One occasion him with his hands around your throat and the next minute you were both naked and from the quick glimpse of me seeing what was going on and now me being a grown man it did not look like you were enjoying yourself a lot and apart from what I witness what he did to you was so wrong,

What you both did to each other was just as bad. You had the car frequently where you could have taken off with us, so I guess I'm no different in that aspect, but back on topic! You both were horrible parents and I think both of you should have never been parents, let alone now you add children into the mix!

I am sorry mum for how everything turned out but in my defense; I was the only child, and he was hurting me so you can see my confusion when you acted like him and I never understood the way you treated me, especially since you are my mum. It never made sense, so why?

Why was I like you? And you could not handle it? Do you know or understand that I was that child tormented by both bullying parents, being the laughingstock in school because I was not like all the other kids as we were poor and I could not have all the nice things that other children wore or played with,

I do however understand now I'm all grown up but seriously people what is fucking wrong with you many people could take this, for example, one of my good friends years ago came for a visit I don't think he was even there for over 30 seconds when all I could hear was mum shouting out tell your friend to go home you have chores to do and to myself, I'm thinking this is not right I have done all my chores so my friend leaves I go up to ask mum what was going on there she stands in the lounge room with a nice piece of garden hose in her hand you know the one she used to flog me with of course there was no valid reason it was mum did not like him and of course,

I swore well you know you should not do that because it's so bad to do that? What about hitting a child? Is that not bad? I'm a little confused about your parenting skills! Yes, there is no book on how to raise a child but I'm pretty sure if there was one it definitely would not be how you downgraded me by whippings by the way you spoke to me or the way you hit me like you were insane?

People who hurt children no matter if it is by hitting them or mentally abuse them by your vile mouth or even worse sexually assault against a child is unforgivable and for the churches not naming any of by names but just to say you use your power of authority all in the name of God well it looks like you're not getting into heaven or maybe you know that there is no God,

No matter the reason there is no reason to hurt a child no reason at all, If you hurt a child I hope you get everything that comes your way like a long jail term or even better let the parents pick the punishment no matter how unhuman it is as those people have taken a child's innocence away from them no one may hurt these children not me not you not your parent's not a Priest not anyone so hands off the children.

Chapter 2 Depression

The Feeling of my depression

I struggle to understand why I've had to live this life the way I have in this kind of mental prison; I struggling so far deep down I'm not sure it can find me. I have been struggling more now that my life is happy! What the fuck is up with that?

I mean really what the fuck is up with that, I've been down spoken to like I am a leper I've seen shit that would curl your straight hair, I'm struggling to find my voice even though I am screaming it's so deafening inside,

I pinch myself it's no damn dream. I now suffer from depression and anxiety. It's more than just the nightmares and PTSD; I don't ask for much. I guess I'd like to be treated like anyone else.

I'm suffering on an epic scale even with what I've been through, I was strong to have made it through the other side still I struggle to forgive me myself for some things that I have done, I should be stronger than I was now I'm just old and sad,

It took my youth from me. I'm struggling because of that fact, now I just sit and wonder what my life would have been? I am so tired I'm afraid I've got no more fight left.

I'll hide in my shell till the sun comes out. It's my only option unless you want me to bleed out?

Depression is horrible I suffer from it myself, depression is a killer it makes you vague it keeps you confused and it also keeps you in a dark place, you feel helpless and you don't feel worthy of anything it makes your head heavy and you don't feel like doing anything;

It is a struggle every day to get out of that headspace that you're in. Depression is a killer. It has killed people and on this day of modern medicine; it is sad to see that so many people suffer this horrible uphill chemical battle.

That is one reason I'm writing this book to get it out there to get the stigma off of the poor people like me who suffer this debilitating condition, when I was younger I would hear about this depression and I used to think what a loud of crap,

look what I've been through and I am fine but years pass and things open old wounds and it is like a floodgate of old hopes and dreams mixed with fear and confusion like a nightmare,

You, know when you wake you once lived that fucked up life and you sit and wonder how you got through it before and I can't even answer that all I know is it hit me like a ton of bricks each brick that fell did so hard and before you know it you are under the wall and you can't get out for me that what depression is like,

Depression can keep you tucked in the one place when you should be way ahead of where you are in your life. It also can make you build walls to help protect yourself because depression is selfish. It wants you all to itself,

I think it gets a little jealous of other people, so it makes you slide down into the deep parts of your mind so it is black and bleak and you shut yourself off from your friends and the world.

When I wrote my first book "Escaping a past" I had to relive the past life that I had lived and it opened some ancient wounds that never healed not back then I become a little more depressed than I had been and I had to relive the murder and being held in a house by my own,

Shame and depression and guilt so reliving the nightmare you may ask what is wrong with me it must have been hard to bring it back up to the surface and so you know I only did it to show people that there is light out there even if you can't see it I am a perfect example of depression might be a killer,

We can survive it if we have support of good friends and family or you just have a robust constitution. Don't let depression hold up your life because we only have one of them.

It is the disease that keeps you miserable you try to fight it and as strong and as mentally strong as I have been in the past it wears you down to where if suicide was as simple as going to sleep just so the pain and suffering would just give you a break just a little break would be nice then sleep you would do,

I know a few people that have admitted to me they suffer it and, of course; we suffer it at a different level of depression. Some people can just shut it out, maybe with a little mental fight,

Me, I struggle with the fight itself and I struggle with tiredness that comes with fighting depression itself and I fear that not enough people are speaking out about it. That's why I am writing about it.,

I don't know how much clearer I can be to say please stop just for a moment and think not for yourself and just think if you had this disease would you not want to help yourself would you not want to shout it from the rooftops and would you not want actual help?

We need to get it out there and make more people aware of this and we need to make medicines available for all people, not just the rich who can afford it, we need to eradicate this disease for the hundreds of thousands of people who suffer this worldwide and it's more than likely in the millions of people across the globe,

For some stupid reason it's a dirty word like o there must be something wrong with that person o what he has a mental illness omg he is probably going to kill someone, no he will not kill someone but you'll judge him all the same like he is a heavy drug addict,

You people who are reading this have no clue what someone goes through the constant struggle to breathe, the fight you have with yourself so no one sees the hell you're living in,

People just look at yourself and you put on that fake smile like everything is ok when it is not and to think how would I put this into words like I'm trying to now, it's like being dazed and confused while the whole time you are sober and clean with no drugs in your system because you don't do drugs no alcohol for a year at least,

Still, the fight is real. It is as real as looking at yourself in the mirror. Have you ever felt like ending it all? Even though life is going well for you, have you ever felt like what would be the less painful way to die because you're sick of the pain that you carry deep down inside, you don't know of a pain-free way?

All you the readers need to know is the fight with depression is very real and if you don't suffer it then you should be great full you don't live like me, depression makes you feel lonely and if you could just lay in bed all day? It seems like a good idea to me!

You can't because you have to give your time and show your face and put on that fake smile so they don't have to deal with the reality that you live in, If I could face depression face to face like a man face to face I would punch you so hard you would not get up from the 4 x 4 that I would hit you,

For good measure I would get right up in your face and tell you with a very strong tone to back the fuck up before I do something that would end in your demise, depression is a bunch of fucked up emotions all rolled into one that no one needs it's a chemical reaction that's not firing on all cylinders,

Some people's depression could be by a chemical mix up while other people's depression comes from a shifty upbringing of bruising violence fueled with your fucked up mental abuse, thinking that's how a man runs his house by screwing with a little boy's mind,

Using violence to get your point across them to top it off, your mother is just as nasty as he is and I think no wonder depression is real, Depression I have suffered with it for more years than I can count the fingers on my hands.

Chapter 3 Religion

Religion is a scam that is my mindset on this chapter I mean for starters look how many are there from Catholic, protestant, Jewish, Islamic, Hindu, masons that's just a few of the many types, ill add my own I've even named it's called "Tonyuism"

Now if there is a God or Gods male or female or even some advanced race that came here millions of years ago and seeded this planet with life, These stores are so old that the only way to believe in any of it is to have faith.

Nothing has happened in the last 2000 plus years to prove that there is a God? Why in the early days God seemed to give hell and grim fire, there always seemed to be some heavenly actions that definitely aid anyone who believed.

 In the times before Christ we believed the Earth was the center of everything, the Sun rotated around the Earth. Now that is God's divine picture, which is a proof that God is real;

We find out that no the Earth is not even close to the center of all things; The sun does not rotate around the earth it is the other way round all our Planets rotate around the Sun and their Moons all rotate around their planet and the Sun rotates around our galaxy our Sun is not even in the center of our spiral galaxy it's in one arm.

if you want to know what God put into the center of our beautiful Galaxy a supermassive black hole nothing can escape it not even light so I guess we should be thankful that when God was telling his people to write this stuff down how could they get it so wrong?

Some people say the hardships people go through are lessons. God is teaching us to be better and doesn't get me started on are all born into Sin, God let his only son die for our sins. Would all be forgiven?

Now that is some fucked up shit? Why would your son need to die for all and every sin committed past present and future all forgiven, God made humans with flaws, the best way I found to have a sweet life is to pray to a God that you can't see and defiantly have faith in the unproven facts of a God that has not been seen by any human except Mosses?

Men and women of the cloth who abuse children for their sexual gratification, is this not alone an act of deadly sinning? The most heinous crime ever?

I am a little confused here. Why would you try to suck people in then tell them you have to rape them, for their sins will be absolved?

Where are the fire and brimstone and smite? The world I would destroy all living things, God said that he flooded the earth to restart again He would never do that aging, I mean people do stupid things sometimes follow a bunch of hypocritical ass holes who say it is this way or that way?

If God is real, I ask any religion to explain to me why would you change the original doctrine? I know we want to have something after we die, Until someone dies and the ghost of that person does an interview with today, tonight or NBC and can share with us the what's and the ifs and what is really after death you have to take at it as a big scam,

The original gods in western culture had three of them: a woman and two men. Then we said there is a woman, all women. Are sinners the fruit of your loins? She commits sins when she has sex,

God had a wife called Asherah we don't known much about her, We will take out one man and one woman and leave us with just the one, At one time in human history, the Greeks and their gods had thousands of what Gods now what is going on? Who is wrong? You right? Am I right or wrong?

How old is God? How could there be Twelve Olympians, Zeus, Hera, Poseidon, Demeter, Athena, Ares, Aphrodite, Apollo, Artemis, Hephaestus, Hermes, and either Hestia or Dionysus?

Or then there is Sumerian they out date all this modern Gods they had a place called the land of the civilized kings, they are the oldest civilization at 3000 BC they had seven gods who are Nanna, Enlil, Inanna, Ninhursag, Anu, Utu, and Enki,

That proves it there we the humans always take from others and add our own bits to make it more sellable.

then you actually have Buddhism, Jainism, Hinduism as the earlier known text of man, so if this is true then it looks like Buddhism and the other two are past and older than normal Jeuss beliefs.

My religion called "Tonyuism" is free to join if you want me to explain it? My simple rules not commands so don't send me money not right now! Or ever! Why? it is free. Yes, it is free!

Me personally I don't think it is fair if you shove what you believe down someone's throat if they think their God is better than your God or Gods rule you must be respectful to others no matter their religion colour, race or creed keep your point of view to yourself if it is disrespectful to anyone keep it to yourself rule,

Read a bible or read a mad magazine just be quite because what I believe you might not agree with so shut your pie hole,

Don't point out that their religion is crap because you think yours is better because clearly if theirs is real they win you lose, so all is well,

Probably the most important rule of all don't use excuses to start a riot and start world war 3 because you read the book it does not say if these people do not convert blow them up and definitely you will have upon entry 21 virgins in heaven I'm sorry but something is wrong if you have to oppose your will on someone!

Fuck it. One more rule for you too the moon. If you defile a child because you're the man you will just be to death, no virgins for you, my friend, as I don't have no secret hide outs for scum like you.,

There is now law starting laying with a woman is the greatest sin of all but to rape a child is ok because they are too young to know and the faith will protect them so my religion is really easy to follow believe what you want,

Don't know even talk about my religion and don't even bother talking about it with other people unless they follow all the rules and there are no children for sale and we don't have a secret handshake and yes the humans are not as smart as we make out we are we all seem to follow what suits us best not what is right and wrong,

Then we recently found the accurate word of Jesus. I did not see we were born into sin? I'm like, how did the church get the bible wrong? I think that is an easy answer. Think about it.,

Jesus the son of God could not have been through Devine intervention the mother of Jesus like all men and women had sex, she was pregnant so starts the big lie because she and her lover would have been stoned to death and that's no made-up story they still do it today and that is because she conceived a child before marriage and if you've read the great book, you would see so much of the real story is missing,

Why would you follow a religion, any religion? The possibility is that Jesus was told by his mother and his stepfather that he, was not conceived, by divine one, remember the son of God is the only person not to be born into sin but we have Noah now he was born into sin but for all the people on earth he was the only one that was good enough and sin-free? be able to see into heaven?

To me, we have a lot of double standards: rich, poor, priest or president. We are all one family, are we not? We are all brothers and sisters, are we not? No religion that I have ever heard of says anything even close to I will smite thy if you not conform to my way of teaching.

Who is more powerful and I'm not saying that there is not a God I would like you to show me how to believe and more so show me you are not hanging onto blind faith because I can't believe with what I have seen and what I been through how could a God let he happen,

Yes, God didn't make the choices as each man's actions are his own and I agree with that, but my problem with that scenario is how being a God all-powerful? all-forgiving? All loving?

If these three things are God, then why are millions across the globe starving? Millions homeless? Under the sanctity of marriage, who do you lose your wife and children and you did nothing wrong?

Why if God is all-powerful and we are talking biblical powerful meaning it's off the planet power also meaning God can change free will to help the ones that are in need but people can't see what I can see,

Let's say I've been told more than once that it has been written in a book all actions all intentions are by a God

Gods Goddess and still nothing is done, so where is God Gods or Goddess? I can tell you it's really simple. We are a simple race of people and we don't look to the past for the. answers we just believe the hand-me-downs given to.us,

The story's that are thousands of years old and some even older remember God appears to Noah or speaks to him and tells him he is going to flood the earth because we as a race are ungodly or unfit to walk this earth so he floods the known world at the time for 40 days and 40 nights it was a biblical rain like no other storm and the boat did not sink but of course you have to have faith,

It tells you that God protected the ark himself and after the known world was flooded, this world should be completely clean because God handpicked the people that were taken on the ark, so how can he get it so wrong?

Reading tonight that the current Pope is going to downgrade the penalties for Priests who get caught doing things they should not be now. These people are God's, people so do they know something we don't?

Like there is no God, or it's not all as we have been told but there is a God, but he didn't do all the things that the bible quotes, We all know from children when telling a story that by the time it reaches its final destination the story now is not even close to the original so now take thousands of years into it and story is no longer valid and when you think about it.

How could any human follow a religion that says well look people are turning away from us so we will force people by burning anyone at the stake for their beliefs especially if they are against the church's interests so that to me is scaremongering to keep you in believing when I see little to no facts to back it up,

Did you know that the son of God Jesus married a sinner? She was a lady of the night. He married her now. Is that not a sin? What if he had a son and I think there are facts out there to say that he got married? He also had a Son.,

Were found in a tomb both his mother and father one brother and himself and his wife and child but no let us keep the lies going I think it is sad to think we are all like sheep having to follow something that we can't see nor hear,

Therefore, I choose to believe in my own and that means Tonyuism is the one for me the rules are simple no question who God is it's what you choose to believe we hold no grudges if your beliefs are not the same as other people, So ill put it in simple words for you these non commandments are rules simple rules for all humans to share

1 if you choose to believe that is up to you and there will be no punishment or banished from your community or to Hell because of it, nor will you be burned to cleanse your sins nor will you be burnt at the stake or even kept captive so no one finds out they are wrong!

2 you won't have your lands taken from you, not even if it is rich in oil or anything else. Why? because it's not mine

3 nor will you be born into sin.

You will just be a sinner if you sin and the sins are:

"Hurting or killing some that is an instant sin,"

"Taking that which is not yours,"

"Selling humans, men, women and children,"

"Kidnapping children and selling them on the black market,"

"Rapping children! women! Men! No matter the reason (being in jail in not a reason)" "attacking people because of their religious beliefs (No matter if they are children men and women)"

"Selling your daughters because they are girls"

"Picking on someone because they are weaker"

"Selling drugs so you can live the good life"

"Making up lies"

"Treating your fellow man with disrespect"

"Keeping anyone as a slave (No matter if it is a sex slave or just someone of colour or non-coloured against their will)",

These rules are not commandments, just basic human rights..

Chapter 4 Rude

I have the freedom of free speech! Right? Or do I not have it at all? This is a serious question? Is it not? What does freedom of speech mean? Does it give me the right to say whatever I want to whomever I want?

Yes, this is true. You can get fucked just because I feel like saying it so. FUCK you. No, then I am confused! So why can't I tell you to go fuck yourself?

Because freedom of speech, the way they penned it down, I think we have misinterpreted it,

That is why! So let me get this right freedom of speech gives you or me the right to have a conversation with someone and not abuse them all just because their views don't fit in with my own? Or yours, so that my friend is freedom to believe in what you want to,

It does not give you the right or me the right to be abusive. No wonder the world is in a messed up place right now and that has a lot to do with many things, but being rude is right on top of that list,

I don't give people the satisfaction of a verbal fight. This shows that I am not only smarter but wiser and stronger;

It does not take much to figure out that being nice makes you feel better and makes for a smoother lifestyle.

Really, who? Is bothered with the constant showmanship of I'm trying to show you I am king shit or me bowing to kiss your ass because you think your shit stinks neither,

Just like the rest of us! I am the boss man and this crap just goes on and on; you know what makes me feel better, not any of that,

I like it when an old lady looks like she needs a hand at the supermarket and you go up and ask would you like something there and she says yes thank you I have been hoping someone would help me I have been trying to grab that bottle of sauce on the top shelf for the last half an hour and you help her out and when you do it and I'm not just saying it but this makes you feel good,

 Or you could just stand there and watch her struggle to grab from the top shelf it is the right thing to do, now does that make you feel all that much more important to watch this?

It does not take Einstein to work out this extremely simple Equation to see with your own eyes just how easy it is to just be nice and the more people that are nice the better the entire world would be and before long the entire world is just that little nicer to be in? Am I right or am I right?

People have taken the freedom of speech out of context by saying what they want to say to whomever they want to in what of the manner they wish. That is not the freedom of speech that is you bending the rules to suit yourself.

You can go to jail for freedom of speech what you want to call it and you can be in the middle of a riot to being in a fistfight and that's because you think you can call someone names to get your point across!

I have a laugh to myself when I watch those TV shows where someone comes in to sell their stuff and the person selling the said items tells the owner that this is what they want and they are not leaving till they get it and I am like what a silly person I would just through you out just for speaking like that and the sure thing he throws them out,

But that whole time they are abusing him for not giving them what they want I mean where do they get off just talking like that in the first place it is rude no matter if you need money and it does not matter what you want it for,

People are just selfish and they wonder why everyone takes a wide berth from that drama, when I got divorced I sold my wedding ring for $20 dollars yes I thought that was a low offer but I did not abuse him for that low offer I went to a few other places who all offered the same deal so I went back and sold it to him with a smile on my face because as much as we have the right to freedom of speech we don't have the right to one abuse them and who knows what is going on in that person's life and they could be having it a lot harder than we are so why be rude?

Knock it off, as it is not right. Does he not have a shop to run? Most likely he has a wife and children to look after or does freedom of speech just give you the right to fuck up someone else's day?

No, it does not Just remember people its freedom of speech, not I can abuse you because the constitution says so when it clearly does not say that it says I may voice my option with respecting other people's rights and believes that my friends are freedom of speech

So stop being a pig and just act like your human if you don't believe me, look up the first amendment! and stop acting like you are a damn feral. That is not how most people have grown up, much better than you are acting!

It's the same as road rage right let's say by mistake you miss judge your change of lanes and by mistake or you did not show your turning lights and you cut someone off, yes it is a mistake but you have a better idea by chasing that person down and abusing them which also may lead you to get into a fight and kill someone all over freedom of speech?

It doesn't sound the same now knowing this, but you still use your Neanderthal mentality because you used the freedom of speech to cover your arse;

I have watched with my eyes rudeness just like many of you have and we all sit back and think, what the hell is going on here you know,

This person is stupid now we don't know the reason he or she is going off but what we know is it sounds horrible it's also made a bad impression on my day and maybe even rub off on me just a little as to be rude myself to the next person who talks to me,

We all should be ashamed of ourself's for acting like that and I am trying to always be the better person and that is what we all need to do.

We need to put others before ourselves,

When you see an old lady think of that lady as your mother or yourself when your that age, would you like to be treated like that I know I would not like it at all and that does not take anyone special to help it also does not take any type of special person to read between the lines and help the old lady out, is that just my way of thinking?

I think if you are just there watching that old lady while you can see she is struggling; I am very disappointed in you.

Paying it forward will always have you coming out on top so remember people stop being rude no matter if you're in the right or not no matter if you don't have the time stop and help that old lady you might just find that you have not just helped an old person but you will find you have just helped yourself!

You also will find that you might just feel a little better because we all know that helping someone else makes life happy and just like it should.

So you see and old person and you see them standing there ask them are they ok do they need a hand, it's truly not that hard to do or is it?. I mean come on people, I could use the C-word right now just to be mean but I'm not going down that road,

But I have used it before I won't lie but I had to learn the hard way that life can't be like this there has to be more than being rude and arrogant like your shit don't stink so people let's stop being rude it does not help anyone it does not help me and it sure does not help you it does not help that person you just flipped the bird to and it's not going to just help you so stop it go get yourself checked if you think that you're in the right and I'm in the wrong,

What if it starts a race war? No, freedom of speech gives you the right to have a conversation with someone and not abuse them all just because their views don't fit in with my own that my friend is freedom to believe in what you want to.

It does not give you the right to be abusive. No wonder the world is in a messed up place right now and that has a lot to do with many things, but being rude is right on top of that list.

I don't give people the satisfaction of a verbal fight. This shows that I am not only smarter but wiser and stronger; it does not take much to figure out that being nice makes you feel better and makes for a smoother lifestyle. really, who could be bothered with the constant showmanship of I'm trying to show you I am king shit; I am the boss man; you know what makes me feel better not being rude, that's for sure.

When an old lady looks like she needs a hand, you help her outright? And when you do, it makes you feel good?

Or you could just stand there and watch her struggle to grab from the top shelf. Now does that make you feel all that much more important to watch this?

It's the same as road rage right let's say by mistake you miss judge your change of lanes and by mistake, you cut someone off yes it is a mistake but you have a better idea by chasing that person down and abusing them which also may lead you to get into a fight and kill someone all over freedom of speech?

It doesn't sound the same now, knowing this,

But you still use your Neanderthal mentality because you used the freedom of speech to cover your ass.

I have watched with my eyes rudeness just like many of you have and we all sit back and think what the hell is going on here you know person is stupid now we don't know the reason he or she is going off but what we know is it sounds horrible it's also made a bad impression on my day and maybe even rub off on me just a little as to be rude myself to the next person who talks to me,

We all should be ashamed of our self's for acting like that and I am trying to always be the better person and that is what we all need to do, we need to put others before our self's and when you see old lady think of that lady as your mother or yourself when your that age,

Would you like to be treated like that? I know I would not like it at all and that does not take anyone special to help.

It also does not take any type of special person to read between the lines and help the old lady out.

Is that just my way of thinking?

Paying it forward will always have you coming out on top so remember people stop being rude no matter if you're in the right or not no matter if you don't have the time stop and help that old lady you might just find that you have not just helped an old person you also will find that you might just feel a little better because we all know that helping someone else makes life happy and just as it should,

When being rude it only makes me feel sad because it is very rare to see someone being rude for it to be justified, for me if you are being rude it tells me you have some type of mental issues or maybe they just have anger issues, either way, they need or is it you just being in control.

Chapter 5 The Meaning Of Life Plus Intermission

What truly is the meaning of life? Look at this when you are young most boys are wreckless endangering their lives for friends either showing off or trying to be the top dog, young girls wanting to be a princess and to dress up like mummy as you get older you start to think of having a family and to make sure you don't make the same mistakes as your parents if you end up having children or you don't, it will all come down to when you're about to hit your middle age this is before 50 you'll be wondering where all the time went there will be for most people some sort of regret some hang-ups some mistakes and you'll start to wonder about the meaning of life and what the hell was all those trials and tribulations about?

Just to get you to a point in your life where you're too old to start over? Is it just no matter how old you get some people will just have a better life than you so what is that all about? What is the true meaning of life I mean the grass bottom roots of it all? Is there a God? If so, which one is the right one? Because we don't want to have a hidden agenda, we just want the truth so what is the meaning of life? Is there a different meaning for everyone or is it universal? Is the meaning of life just life? Maybe it has no actual meaning maybe it's we are born to one day die and if we are lucky the meaning of life is just around the corner? Could the meaning of life be found in happiness? Could it be seriously found being in love? Could it be found if you were to die? What about a hard lesson to learn could the answers be there? Why is the true meaning of life so hard to find? If you walked a mile in my shoes would you find it before me? Maybe there is no meaning at all maybe we just live, and we just die? Maybe there is no God or Gods? Maybe it's in mediation? What about landing on the Moon did they find it there? Maybe the meaning of life is just that a paradox unto itself? Is it in getting your hands dirty? Is it when you help an old lady cross the road? What about looking deep into someone's eyes the windows to the soul would we find it there?

The meaning of life must be something huge and magnificent it must be grand not something so simple and simplistic don't you think? What about when we dropped the bomb did, we get it then? What about the dinosaurs when they were here 65 million years before us could there be an answer in that for everyone? What about every action has equal opportunities for an opinion or reaction of indifference? It could be in that pot of gold at the end of the rainbow. Or in a near-death experience? What about being kind to everyone? Or what about where the wind blows? Could it be having the key to someone's heart? What if the meaning of life has us seriously searching for something that is either not real or something lost so long ago? Can the meaning of life be found when you're stoned or when you're so blind drunk you can't see 1 foot in front of you? Is it in the fresh flowers I can smell? Or is it in the sentence that I speak? When all is said and done do you have the answer right in front of you the meaning of life?

Is it in the fact that you get under my skin? Or is it more along the lines of being like the Deli Lamar? Could it be in watching the stupid TV? Or is it in missing someone who has passed? Does it even matter is that we're it lies? Could it be in this rant somewhere? Could it be in your favorite numbers? or could it be in the reflection looking back at me? Or could it be in my great vocabulary of very bad swearing? I know there are meanings in every sentence in every life that is born I know there are meanings in pain, love, and loss so what is the actual meaning of life?

I was thinking again trying to go to a deeper level! an understanding of this ancient history that goes back thousands of years with many before me contemplating the actual meaning of life you know the one thing that legend has it that soothes your whole soul you know your whole being, I know a lot of people put their faith in a God or Gods and they seem to be fulfilled or are they? I know a time when I believed but I never had that feeling of greatness why is that? either the meaning of life has a different meaning for everyone? or it's the same if it is the same then the only conclusion I can draw from that is the meaning of life has nothing to do with God or Gods so that leaves me with one other different meaning for me than it does for you or does it? I have searched my feelings Hight and low deep and shallow! and for me, I can only come up with being in true love not loving someone I mean deep true love which I have felt only once before in my 50 years and to be truthful it was the only time in my life that I was soothed from that moment I felt like I had no depression or any anxiety? is it even possible? I mean is it possible truly possible in any type of dimension? All I had was this deep happiness like I could not be touched by anything and the only thing that could take me off that high was her no longer wanting anything to do with me, she was the only thing that could bring me down! so is it the true meaning of life being in love? true and pure love? or am I fooling myself? is it possible that there could be something else stronger something else that can soothe the heart mind body and soul? I would like to explore this even deeper, I am lost to think of something that could be stronger and more effective, maybe for me the meaning of life is being in love? what is the meaning of life for you? let us just hope that we all can find the meaning for ourselves as I don't think there is a one fits all meaning of life I think that being happy in your own heart and your mind is clear of regrets and your soul is at true peace then I think we will find the meaning of life, wellbeing and long-lasting happiness I think is the key to each one's salvation and without that the true meaning of life will never be found, I think the things to defiantly avoid to find the true meaning of life are as follows but not in any order Gossip, Fighting, Hating, Resentment, Religion keeping it to yourself, Selfishness, Selfishness, Not listening, Forcing your beliefs onto other people, Lies, Starting a war, Forcing yourself on someone man women or child, Using your power to, Using religion to get your way in the world no matter what the reason, Killing people in the name of religion sickness me.

Intermission

Overwhelming damnation the kind that leaves you cold and all alone the kind that keeps you hidden from the big world outside it keeps you scared from people that might judge you it's the kind that has you on your knees begging, pleading, praying for a God any God to listen to you, An Overwhelming presence of fear knowing that miracles won't and don't happen here There's a meticulous way that it all works it's all overwhelming to me there's just no support from God or mankind can't you see, The overwhelming feelings that are deep down inside never leave there seems to be no care left in the world not even for little old me!

Crazy days and even crazier nights that I was living

I somehow got a second chance at breathing

Not a lot of people had any type of faith in me

Something just snapped deep down inside of me

I screamed and shouted out loud

I can't point a finger at any one thing

Now I am living without faith or fear

I can see so very clear more than you can know

Now it is sad, but it is true some of the lengths that some people will go too

That's ok I know wrong from right I bet you can sleep at night

I guess you will have to fight your fights from now on

I felt like I was locked in a cage I am not any type of Bird?
so go figure that anyway

At one time or another, I believed in a God that did not
exist

Could you just think how I might have felt knowing there
was no help outside

Even within the side of me I tried everything in sight guess
now I will have to know my rights?

If I go down the wrong path of my life it must be karma
setting in?

I have no secrets too bare or share with you what about
you?

This life is no game when other people's lives are at stake ?

Think before you speak my Mum would always say

It's a pity that your life is one big crying shame.

Time stands still I sit and ponder my mind walks about
Time mistakes wonder Can't take back time can't change a
thing can't stop that clock from ticking I feel blue it
happens a lot I wish I could turn back that fucking clock! I
wonder what might have been I feel stilly just saying these
things Can't take back time Can't change a thing Can't stop
that clock from ticking The world keeps moving! Many
years have passed Others have moved on Wish I could

change these things Can't take back time Can't change a thing Can't stop that clock from ticking Can't go back can't take it back Wish I could change these things The clock keeps ticking can't stop it Wish I could though sad how time goes Can't take back time Can't change a thing Can't stop that clock from ticking Time change wishful thinking Faster, slower no change though Many nights dreaming many things Still can't change a God dam thing Can't take back time Can't change a thing Can't stop that clock from ticking Wounds heal slowly Time keeps its own pace No matter the situation Time is never late Can't take back time Can't change a thing Can't stop that clock from ticking Fates warning No matter what you do Throughout all of the ages Time it self keeps its own clock Can't take back time Can't change a thing Can't stop that clock from ticking Can't stop that clock from ticking Can't change a thing Can't take back time.

The sea of madness

Your life is on the edge it's out of control what a mess it's become

Time wasted on memories that should have long been forgotten

The sea of madness is here to stay the sea of madness can go either way

The sea of madness the sea of madness

The darkness is calling you again calling out your name loud from afar

Slipping over falling into the abyss it grows darker by the day

The sea of madness is here to stay the sea of madness can go either way

The sea of madness the sea of madness

I drink the elixir from the fountain of youth a whiskey pure damn straight

I'm sinking in the quicksand of hate-fuelled by my blindest

The sea of madness is here to stay the sea of madness can go either way

 The sea of madness the sea of madness

A love turned so bad that Nostradamus would not have prodicted

The days are filled with an emptiness that can't seem to be filled

The sea of madness the sea of madness the sea of fucking madness.

Waves of darkness surround my thoughts inwards I hide protecting the memories that made me happy once' protecting my heart as I go deeper' I travel deep into my soul hiding from the ghosts of my past building the walls thicker and higher as I go' I never trusted my instincts I felt it for sure' I decided to ignore them and go on with the love that made me feel whole and complete I was burnt beyond all belief, You took my heart and destroyed me completely I never thought it would happen to me' I've never felt such pain or so much anguish before in my life I wanted you and I waited for you to see the error of your ways I forgave you but you never forgave yourself for what you did to you us and me now that is a huge shame.

I'm off-center in this huge world, My beat if off tilt by just a little, I'm so tired my brain is not active

My head is not in the right space

I've forgotten more than I can remember I've drunk more than most could

I've seen things that would fry your brain

I've been beaten again and again

I'm off-center in this huge world

My beat if off tilt by just a little

I'm so tired my brain is not active

My head is not in the right space

Who would care if I was gone? Who would dare talk about such things?

Who were my true friends? Who will hold the candlelight?

I'm off-center in this huge world

My beat if off tilt by just a little

I'm so tired my brain is not active

My head is not in the right space

If only you could see what I see! Does anyone care out there?

If only I had a dollar for every time you didn't care! Does caring exist in any place?

I'm off-center in this huge world

My beat if off tilt by just a little

I'm so tired my brain is not active

My head is not in the right space.

I've drunk a lot of whiskeys to kill the pain of a stupid divorce one I might add I never wanted but it was all because you could not keep your hands to yourself, I mean you did make a promise to be mine for richer or poorer for better or worse you took my love and turned it on its head you made it dirty you made a fool of me you left me to die without a fucking care, You even asked me way before you had an affair to not hurt you and not to hurt the children but it was you that did both,

you could have saved my heart as it feels like I'm condemned to some sort of Hell but no you just played me, made up lies to save yourself, You even turned it around and made me look like I was the one that did it but because I loved you I said nothing to save you the one I've loved all these years,

I took it hard on the chin like a man! then you had the gall to stop me from talking to the children and that was because you wanted it to all go away and the eyes would stop looking your way I lied to everyone and said my brother had cancer that's why I had to leave even though you lied to CPS I did to try and keep the family unit together while you were ripping it apart,

Did i do the right thing? it haunts me to this day now i have no family no brothers at least i lost it all on some random event the type that kicks you in the fucking head, only if you did the right thing i would not be an author right now maybe its meant to be maybe i was meant to lose it all so i could say somneone else its not the first time or the secound maybe ive got more people to save who knows who cares do you?.

I've written two books over 1000 poems and songs and counting.

A heartbroken man trying to crawl forward out of this dark pit

Weighted down by past mistakes could any of them changed things

I'll pick myself up off the floor it's hard when your heart is breaking

I've been trapped in memories for years I wonder how you
are today I still do

I never asked for this I was good to you was I not? there is
only one fool here, burning in my madness flashes of our
time together flashes passes me yes its me the fool,

You turned up the heat on my heart it would have stayed
intact I know

I begged and pleaded to try and save our marriage, you
tossed us on the floor like I was a used condom or
something

I'm not sure if you were truly hurting or was that your
lying eyes but did you think about what I wanted? What i
was even feeling?

I did not even get a say that still saddens me

I said fuck the world and the excuses I'll take it all on if I
must

You shut me down shut me off if I mentioned love, you'll
stop talking

I'm confused for better or for worse was that not the deal?

For richer or poorer through good times and bad i must
have signed a diffrent contract?.

you left me high and dry begging for more, I felt for a few
short days after your lover took off that you started to
come back towards me was that just another fucking game

of yours? Either way, it makes no difference, the thing that gets me the most is I could feel your love and when you saw me hurting I genuinely could see that you were sorry but none of that matters now it was a long time ago and I'm just getting this off my chest no matter what comes from it this had to be said to set the record straight no matter the words are written here and no matter if you hate me or still love me I still love you always have, what I've said is the truth and yes it fucking hurts still.

If I could go back in time! man, I know what I would do and yeah, I would end up in jail for murder, not an author that I am now, I know people say that time changes many things and maybe it does but for some reason, that door for me is still open and I know given time with you I know the spark, Time is a fickle thing either way WF has no real clue just how lucky he really is my time over again id do it all the same the only change id be waiting behind a bush or a tree and he definiottly would not got to driven away with you i would of caved his skull in omfg the shit he said to me are you real? guess whi is fucking your wife now! knowing that i could not do anything now this is mwrong on so many points but my point to you and WF if i could of got my hands on him both our lifes would be diffrent not just because im angry at what he has done and yes that has made me super anagry and then to say that with photos attactched! Still the point of the matter is he would of been a dead man and i would at least feel better because he would not be having that chance with you and when i got out of jail you might know and understand just the leankths that i would go to,

WF is a weak minded piss ant who only had his with with you because he was no man was not then is not now will never be in the future, do i hate him yes why may you ask? really your gonna go there? OMFG he is a dirt bag doushe o what it is only right in his mind because the only tet you thought i would see would be is O you should be straight with him and tell him we are together? Damn but this little weak ecuess of a man sent it through tet not to my face, are you not taking my wife? then man up? show me how large your balls are? o thats right little mans balls! you only felt tuff behind your phone or in your car down the block you could not face me man to man what the fuck was i expecting a man? no not a man a person that looks like a man but acts like a child and played games because his balls had not dropped yet, yes i still have that challage up come face me? or all face you? name the time and place becuase WF your fucked if you ever go in the right with me, Id hunt you down like a wilter beast and hit yo so hard you would have to shit for a week to find your fucking teeth, no i dont want money and fame i just want you to pay for what you did to me and im pretty sure i know two other men that would take a shot at you if you where game enough!

Chapter 6 UFO And Conspiracy

We start of this rant about UFO's and the possible chance that we are not alone in the universe, when you think of a UFO you think little green men from mars, now for a start personally I think that if we are not alone then we have a higher chance of these creatures being more like star wars than little green men but anything is possible, Take a look back in time now to the very late 1800s were I might add a UFO crashed and the occupant died from their injuries now the conspiracy part of this problem is it was not until the early 1900's that we had a flight with the right brothers a not very flight worthy of great height's or distance so what crashed the crash? So, either we have a real spaceship that crashed, or we had humans first flight way before the 1900's so which one is it?

Then we move to a much later time 1947 to be precise were a UFO had crashed in the desert now as the story goes their where at least 4 body's approximately 4ft tall 3 of them died due to their injuries but one lived and was walking around true or not true? So you have many people that arrive and they see what was described as a disc-shaped object badly damaged now the military turn up and take over but the strange thing is they tell the reporters that it was a flying disc that crashed now why would the military say that when one it was just a weather balloon even if it was extremely important to keep it a secret and I am pretty sure most people could tell what looked like a disc-shaped object, so why tell the UFO story to the press if the only latter to say about their top secrets weather balloon so which one is it UFO or weather balloon? You decide,

For me it comes down to no matter if it is real or not you just have to look at the facts ok let's say that every UFO sighting is a top military project why would they land on in a school ground in Australia where it was seen by hundreds of people that's a bit silly don't you think? Or the big one just recently a big triangle UFO why would you let this be seen by not just the surrounding people but for it to be picked up on TV for the next lot of new Stuff? Now I'm not saying that it is a stunt by aliens or humans to sway you to believe or not to believe in one or the other I'm saying this is what I see now it's up to you to say yes that makes sense or your just a wacko author of this book, This might be true but there are many cultures out there that have recorded strange lights in the sky some even date back 1000,00. thousand it's in artwork dating back way before a man could fly the first plane made by the right brothers in 1903 so how could there be any kind of craft flying around even 100 years before that or even a 1000 plus years how is this possible? when both facts are easy enough to get hold of so do your research and send me an email if you find damming proof that UFO's are not real so go do your research and I don't mean the first thing you read go deep and try and find the true you might be surprised.

I have seen strange lights in the sky now was it a secret military aircraft? Was it a UFO? I see in the night sky two balls of light they constantly stayed the same distance apart moving left to right up and down zig zagging all over the sky they were moving quite fast then they would slow down I'm looking at this thinking I wonder what it could be not saying it's one of the other than after a few minutes it just shot up and incredible speed there was no sound so what was it? You decide! It's always hard to say yes I seen this and that from one person's point of view when we all could be wrong and if this is all a hoax by the governments around the world why would they hoax I understand the backlash from religions all over the world and if that is the case why to let them be seen not just by one but thousands so you can see why I might be a little confused,

Then you have leaked video of a UFO built by the military looks like it can barely get off the ground so how did they get them up so high when it looked like it could not even fly? And if this was a hoax why would they go to the lengths to build one to leak the video out so we can believe that UFOs are real? That to me makes no sense whatsoever so what would be the point behind leaked photos of one nation trying to make one? Was it because maybe after recovering one they could not figure out the technology, so they wanted to build them self-one? I mean you could easily come up with 10 just as valid reasons is to why they made one the same as the crashed UFO 10 other reasons it's possible or covered up its just crazy, It's always hard to say yes I seen this and that from one person's point of view when we all could be wrong and if this is all a hoax by the governments around the world why would they hoax I understand the backlash from religions all over the world and if that is the case why to let them be seen not just by one but thousands so you can see why I might be a little confused,

Why is it so hard to believe that another species just as smart or even in space much smarter could exist? what area in the night sky could host such beings? Such life that is so far away they would have to know how to bend space and time at will and of course no one or nothing is smarter than humans as we are so backward in thinking like say the closest star is 20 light-years away it would take 20 light-years to get to earth and 20 light-years to get home that's 40 light-years in total so that would sound a little farfetched, we can only hope they can figure it out before I'm too old to witness it I want to know do they fly how fast can they travel and can we go faster the speed of light? If so, how much faster can they go? Do they have mother ships? How big are they? Can they travel at the speed of light? Is it like Star Wars? Teaming with all types of exotic plants and animals and if there is life in other words? we just have not found them that does not mean they are not real we are just too sheltered and also too stubborn to think outside the box before we can't turn back the clock and look after the earth it's the only home we have for now until we can learn how to start a new planet even if that means making a new home,

There is a theory out there that says we did not come from here and that is possible our early cells that would start over millions of years what ended up with is a rock that bounces off of another planet or even another rock and it lands here and seeds the life that we know call home so under that conclusion there would be another planet out there at least hosts life and no matter if I believe that earth is not the only planet to host any form of life and to think that we have the only planet that can host life shows our true arrogance on how cocky we think we are no wonder the aliens don't want to come here why would you want to come to a planet where most likely they would nuke you as soon as you land.

flat earth conspiracy this is one of the biggest and most stupid conspiracies of all time it's as bad as saying a UFO was a Weather balloon or Swamp gas or even a Radar reflector or you come up with the Moon landing was fake, The flat earth conspiracy is so far wicked I know it came in a time when we thought the stars where lights hanging like it was on the ceiling and I just wonder why that has not taken off like the flat earth has, I mean how crazy is it truly? look at it like this they don't doubt that all of the other planets are round and our moon and sun are also round so why is the Earth flat? I also saw one very good piece of fact? that points to the Earth is round and the flat earthers believe and I think because back when the map of the known world they believed it was flat and they also believed that they would full off the edge of the world but some very smart people came up with their theory upon doing their experiments and with each one said the world was a globe and the churches did not want to know because that was heresy, they had to keep their secret, who would know what would have happened but to me it is clear the world is a globe not a globe with the top half cut off, I think you would be hard pressed to find any person that has done their schooling to say that the earth is flat plus I can't even see why you would even believe it too began with, with all the videos I have watched and all the flat earthers have not even given me one fact that proves otherwise because we all say you need to back up what you're saying not with some lose beliefs that did not stand up then let alone now,

Another conspiracy is a story from the bible take Noha's big boat and how it rained for 40 days and 40 nights! the biggest problem I have with this one let me take you on a ride now close your eyes and listen to what I am saying, You have this boat that's made of just wood now he gets all the animals from the world the problem back then it was only the known world right? let's say that it was the whole world! so Noha take his family gets them to travel to all parts of the world and to get each animal a male and female know that would take so much time? and then you have the boat built all animals all aboard and then comes this biblical rain now do the math it rains so hard that the whole world floods now the highest peak on earth is Mount Everest at just over 29,000 ft, So let's take 29,000ft and the whole globe covered to at least 29,000ft this much water for one would as in rain would have flooded the boat but let's again say ok the earth was flooded to at least 29,000ft at this altitude there is little to no oxygen so most of the animals would have died also including the humans on the boat so I guess to say that you have little food a biblical down poor not a lot of oxygen they all would have died plus when the boat makes landfall some 40 place days later it would have crashed into some mountain killing any remaining animals and humans and also there would have not been any humans to great or that would have survived that amount of water so no humans no animals so how did they survive? take into again the rain the altitude no food no fresh water no oxygen and half the animals would of ate the ones that would of died before the lack of oxygen killed the rest also means killing all humans on board, and if you have ever seen a body of water that sits across the road and say its only 1 or 2 feet in depth now it sits there for days before we see it slowly go down so explain it to me how at the whole world is covered in water to at least 30,000ft after a 40 day and night down poor and it just disappears in a matter of moments because it would have to as there would not of been enough food for 40 days let alone the months it would of taken for the water to have gone down far enough for the boat to hit land now they say that they have found it in a country called Turkey and it is just about 3700ft at sea level now if the math says you need up to 30,000ft of water to cover the whole Earth and now after 40 days and nights and clearly now the water level has to hit at least down to 3000ft that's 27,000ft from sea level water covering the whole glob how long do you think it would take for the water to drop enough for it to hit land clearly it would have to be months if not years! so tell me, dear believers, how do you make me believe that the water dropped like undoing a plugin a bath makes me understand how you see that after knowing some real facts and after doing some reading they have worked out that they were on the ship for more than a year, so the bible has one big ass lie, you are the judge! then, of course, you have the Yeti, Loch Ness monster, Giant humans, Alien abduction, Top secret government black budgets, Flight 19, The Philadelphia experiment, Men in black, Area 51, That's just to name a few.

Chapter 7 LGBTQIA+

People who are born this way they are born, no wait a minute it is the devils work the devil himself hand picks the sperm that's going to impregnate your healthy holly god fearing woman life because you never had sex before marriage and you even go to church every Sunday so why is your son gay I'm just saying because what your telling me is that it is the devils work, I mean really people do you truly believe that? Wow well this is where my freedom of speech comes into play because I don't believe in that what you're selling saying at least, it is not something that they see on TV it is not your Mother that kissed her best female friend on the cheek that turned you, you did not change your mind when you became an adult it's in your DNA you fool and I suppose if you want to believe it the other way and when it comes to God that's why Popes and Cardinals molest little boys wow what wait a minute they are not going to Hell? Holly shit balls batman we have a double standards here but us dumb asses can't see it in the early days Popes had wife's they had to change that when they reread the good old book that states the woman's womb is were evil starts that's why there is a marble statue of a woman that is covered up because that alone will turn you into a bad person and maybe even turn a woman to be gay where every person born has the true natures call when they become adults to find a partner to breed it is not a sin nor will it turn you bad because you have a child out of wedlock all these silly rules are to keep you giving to the church and slowly people are starting to move away from the churches and why do you think that is?

I myself am not gay or bi sexual but I do believe in fair and equal rights for all people no matter the colour or religion beliefs it's that same dogma that keeps the human race from not moving to the next level of our universal ranging, People today are a little more giving then in the 50's and 60's but still we treat gay people like second class people like they have the black plague or something what is wrong with you people we allow the churches to practise their old ways and there is no love there just rape of young boys but this is ok? But have here two people who are born to like the same sex and they don't join a religion to hide the fact that they like same sex relations so why can love win out is this not gods will love it's all about love? O I must have been mistaken to think that what you do is hidden by the churches of the world but you can let two people who have nothing but true love in their hearts for each other and you say no it's a sin so we can condone that? I am confused on the way you rule things, is not love beautiful? Isn't love kind? Is this not what true marriage all about? And I think I'll throw in my two cents in for good measure, I think if we let gay people marry I would think there would be less divorces? And if you look back in time we have had some pretty cool famous gay people like Freddy Mercury as an example what a beautiful soul he had and his sexuality did not make him famous his voice did so politicians and men of the cloth please tell the people why we have to follow you when a gay person falls in love it is the same as a man and woman, I have some gay friends and I tell you they are better than some of you straight cats who force your lifestyle on us normal folk we are not like you and just for the readers here if you have an open mind you will know that there are some gay people in parliament but for ridicule they stay gay behind closed doors but they are still gay all it is we just don't know that they are and if they came out you would find most of the Australian people would support them but most of these people are old school they might be gay but they are married and see their lover in secret,

For me I'm not bothered if you are gay bi sexual or straight because when your sexual oration is I can tell you it's not my business because it's your life and you should be free to choses if you want to be with a man or a woman, and of course what would be worse than being gay? Being gay and being interracial a black woman with a white woman or a white man with a black man or even mix it up and have a black woman with an Asian man or a black man with a white Greek woman now that is no different than your relationship with your husband who is playing around or even a true story for you once long ago a couple where going to get married now the woman knew something was up so she left work and went home early and just walked in and she caught her partner with another man now she did not know that he was bi sexual right now another true story I knew a guy who was playing around on his partner now he got caught and she left him so out of those two stories which one was the worst? I can tell you both are the same two different relationships both relationships ended in a disaster so the basic moral of the damn story is it had nothing to do with she was punished because her husband liked both men and women and the other took a woman so no gayness or bi sexual activity's going on there this is what the hatters will tell you that someone who is gay or bi sexual that they are evil then so is the guy who played around on his wife what does it make him? It's clear and simple to me there is a clear agenda by the governments of the world and the fanatics of religion to keep true people that love each apart from getting married because of their own twisted views and beliefs.

Chapter 8 Cars

Cars

Cars don't get me started with cars o dear wow cars I've had a few over the years let's start with my first car it was a 1964 EH Wagon Auto it's colour was a mustered it was completely stock standard and I purchased it after my mate had ran it into a ditch, it basically only needed cosmetics bonnet both front guards grill and stone tray, this was my first time doing any of this I'd never removed any part of a car before by the end of it I had cuts and bruises but I now had some understanding on how it all went back together, the poor old girl now had a right hand white guard the left hand one was a dark blue the bonnet was a brown the stone tray and grill was a light blue in colour I was proud as punch to be driving it around even though she was multi coloured in the end I sold it to buy an EH Sedan which is mentioned next and who I sold it to was the same guy I brought it off originally as he told me he wanted to get into mowing lawns and stuff I said that's a cool idea, I latter found out that he cut the back half off and turn that part into a trailer but both front and back ended up at the tip, I would of never of sold it if I knew, foolish things we do when we are younger,

Another friend of mine had a 1963 EH Sedan light blue in colour it had an Aussie 4 Speed now this thing could fly and she could hold onto a corner like she was on rails that was before I brought her when I got her the linkage for fist gear was broken and the engine was tired so when I picked her up I got her back to my place and before I was going to put in the shed I thought I could smell like plastic was burning so I turned her off and waited for it to cool down so like an hour had past I opened the bonnet and there was a few wires just hanging so I unplugged the battery and reconnected them and went to put on the positive terminal and sparks flew out and burnt my fingers as I've tuned my back to the car sucking my fingers the engine bay had caught fire I knew to close the bonnet to smother the flames which it did again once it had cooled down I looked at the damage and it had burnt the main part of the wiring loom so all I could do was to put in the shed were she sat for a long, time years had passed and I had to move so I sold it to a friend for $400.00 dollars on the condition that if it was ever for sale I could buy her back deal was done I moved and not long after I hear some horrible news about her so I went for a look and low and behold it was true she was on its roof, Windows smashed parts had been torn off and of course the best two piece were missing the wide HR wheels with EH hubcaps and the diff and front end where missing, yes you can imagine I was pissed off but it was his car after all now he did pay for it,

A friend of mine had a Valiant charger, now this thing took some punishment in the end but when he brought her she was in good nick for her age, if I remember correctly he was putting in a stereo doing all the wiring and when he was done he went to move her out of the driveway and the passenger side door was open he did not see so as he backed out yes you can guess what happened yes the door peeled backwards and it was completely stuffed he ranted and shouted as it was everyone's else's fault not his but anyway we end up getting the door to close with a lot of banging, next thing you'll think this guy is crazy him and another friend of his are out the front coming up the street playing let's see how close we can get to each other but of course there was no hit and miss, up and down the street they go changing sides so both sides were completely smashed up like a smash up derby, I never found out why they did that but it was their own cars not mine lol, Another friend of mine had brought himself a nice WB Panel Van she was a 1981 model it was white in colour it was stock as a rock car for his work, when he was changing jobs so he got a new paint job also white she looked really good after a few years it needed some mechanical work doing to her so I give her new oil new air filter new points new spark plugs new leads and after about an hour she was done so I said to him take her for a spin which he went and came back he said she is running like a dream,

when he finally was leaving he backed it out and as he put her in first gear she started to pop and fart and bang she just stopped in the middle of the road, he was desperately trying to start her she was firing it would not start my friend gets out slammed his door and he has no mechanical knowledge what so ever, well he was carrying on outside the front of my house swearing f this and f that and I said look let me see if I can figure it out well as I was trying to see what wrong he was having a go at me saying that it must of been my fault because the car was running fine, I asked him to try and start it so I could hear what was going on, he did as I asked he cranked her over and everything sounded like it should, he gets out of the car while I've still got my head in the engine bay he start saying I knew I should of taken it to a professional, then he starts ranting about how he is going to smash his car with a hammer I asked him to simmer it down a bit as it was in my street I had to live there so he tells me that I can get nicked and I said look mate if your hell bent on smashing her let me give you a hand I shouted at him and as I walked off to get a hammer he goes where are you going?

I said to grab a hammer he said don't be stupid I said look you can't come into my street abuse me after I fixed your car and expect me to be all chilled out and low and behold he tells me that I need to be quite I said no this is my street I'll shout if I want to not you and I get in the car I can hear when I try and start it from in there as I turn the ignition I hear her turn over again it sounds normal I said to him are you sure this thing has enough fuel in it he said yes I'm like well unless your fuel gauge is not working she is on empty he goes get out and let me have a look, yes low and behold it is empty we put fuel in yes she started straight up and sounded just like she should,

A friend of mine brought a hot rod EH a 1964 model she was a nice old girl she was candy apple red in colour when he brought it but he wanted it to be perfect so he could enter it into car shows and win trophies, bit by bit I started to strip it down numbering as I went along so I knew what came off what side of the car and I needed to do this also because some things had to be replaced like the strips on the doors so I've got it down to a bare shell and I mean no one bolt not one wire, it was taken to be sandblasted so all ready for the fisher oil to go into those hard to reach places, I stripped the front end and diff to its bare shell and they were sandblasted as well they were then sent off to be dipped in chrome, once they came back it was all new ball joints tie rods sway bars the works, my friend was wanting to keep the candy colour but he wanted it to stand out so people would know it was his car not the guy who owned it before, I said well why don't you pick a new candy colour and he could not decide I said look this one here looks really nice it was called candy brandy wine and that's the colour he went with, she has now been sprayed in that colour doors are all fitted front and back end in a set of old wheels put on the ones that he wanted to use, the engine and box are being fully rebuilt the car is now a rolling body so it goes back to his house where I fit all the bits and pieces door trims seats seat belts dash glove box so forth and so forth, the wheels have been put on a lathe and are super smooth and looking brand new the engine and box are done now all fitted, it was then taken to the mechanic to tune it now she is ready to go, he gives it the all clear and he drives it away, he did let me drive it once and it was a dream to drive and I'm glad that he let me do all that I did because he knew I knew what I was doing,

One of my favorite cars that I've owned was a 1979 HZ GTS Ute when I brought her she was only missing the distributor so that's ok, I drove it said yes I want it right in front of me the distributor was taken out so I knew it was an easy fix I got her home on a trailer and I had to wait a few weeks before I could get one so two weeks have passed and I get a distributor I put it in and fire her up nope nothing it won't start, I check the points gap perfect I check the fuel half a tank so that's ok I look at the leads and spark plugs because sometimes they just go and nope they are all good so after I checked everything over I tried again it turns it cranks you can see it wants to start but nope so I had to get a mobile mechanic to come out he said it might be this and it might be that and he had the parts on his so all good, he started it and I said o I see it's your coil so he replaced it nothing fuel pump nothing starter motor nothing he said well in all my years I've never had this problem so I'm like great I paid $1500 for it and she won't start so she sat in the shed for a few months and I'm thinking to myself I know I'll just save my money and buy a new engine because something is clearly wrong with it, A friend of mine came around on this day that I decided to push her out of the shed to give her a de web and a wash my friend says do me o I see you've got it going I said nope I don't he goes crank her over for me I said mate I'd love to but the battery is dead he said that's ok put it back in and I'll jump start you so I did that he hooked me up and he said now fire her up and keep cranking it till I say stop I'm like ok mate I crank her over and he has his head under the bonnet I can see he is moving side to side he crabs a screwdriver and buts it up against the engine block he puts his hand out and waves for me to stop the engine, he goes I know why it won't start mate you have three bent push rods and a leak in your head gasket so they got replaced and boom fired straight up, I drove it for s time until this one day maybe 6 months later I pulled up at the lights and the police were right behind me and I'm like just take it easy off the lights and they won't pull you over light turns green as I just get it around the bend the engine let's go a whole lot of smoke the engine just blew up here is the blue lights flashing so I pulled over he put on my car a red sticker but he aloud with his escort to drive it home which was only a few minutes up the road and I kept looking out the back window and it was just a huge plume of smoke so when I got her home she sat there till I got s new engine for it,

After all that time the person whom I was sharing a place with said I have a good idea and it will save you money I'm like yes that sounds good she well you know I'm a pensioner let me put your Ute in my name and that will get you cheaper registration I thought well it's not a bad idea at the time but it was a really stupid idea so he's the Ute was now in her name cheaper registration for me a bonus so I was ready to get out of that places I told her I was leaving to go overseas to get married she said well you can't take the Ute it's in my name and if you drive it away I will have you charged with theft and she stuck to her guns she would not let me have my keys so I lost my pride and joy even though I would of had to sell it but that's not the point she used me and told me lies, My now car is a 1994 White VR Holden Ute V6 5 Speed Manual I brought it from a car yard for $4,300 she has been pretty reliable I've made some changes from the original car that I brought it now has VZ Monaro wheels, handmade bonnet scoops, a Ned Kelly bonnet emblem a Ned Kelly helmet diff cover, I've replaced the dash with a VS dash and it has blue dash lights of a night, I've put seats from a VS Sedan and Door trims from the same car, I really want to put a supercharger from a Monaro in it and Monaro seats because they are so comfortable but that is in the future some time I hope, She has blown a puff of smoke here and there and it was getting a little worse as the months wore on so I took her to the mechanics and he said it's just the valve stem seals and I said if that's what it is do it so she went in and had the job done and it has not blew a puff of smoke since so now it's back to cruising and I was thinking if you live in Queensland and you own a Holden Ute or Holden 2 Door Monaro Coupe come join me at Australian made Holden Utes and 2 Door Monaro Coupes Queensland, we do cruises and we are a pretty good bunch of guys and girls we are just about to at the time of writing this are doing a cruise for my cousin who has cancer and if you're interested come join also from this cruise all cruises after that will be in her memory so thank you for reading and joining if you're in Queensland because we are a Queensland based car group only i ended up selling it to buy a VS Ute, I got The VS Ute in 2019 for a good price $500.00 the only problem with her was a blown auto which I replaced but I knew it was blown so that was ok she was pretty much stock apart from the wheels and the rear bars in the tray so to make her a little more mine I pulled her into the shed and started to make some mods to her my favored one would have to be the 1969 Pontiac bonnet scoops which I molded in myself I was quite proud of myself and through the months I'm got two sets of wheels one lot are off a BMW 9inches on the front and 10inches back and the other pair are off a 2005 Monaro damn she looks so good i have a mate of mine who is going to give her a lick of paint in her original colour Alaskan white, the scoop inserts are handmade by me in red the seats are coming out and VZ leather seats are going in to it the seats are so comfy I also made my own 3d Ned Kelly helmet pultruding out of the tailgate molded by me, I've gone with a small amount of red in the scoops and a few other spots she has a few hidden compartments I got a nice stereo for her then sad news i sold her in hard times now i wait till i have a 2002 2003 CV6 Monaro in any colour,

I also believe that Holden our car here in Australia made a huge mistake and in the end, it screwed them over 1st When Holden brought back the Monaro name plate after 24 years and the ads were also very good they decided to take it to Bathurst our nations premium racing car track they would make a race car and a road going version of the racecar now in 2002 the mighty Holden Monaro would take on in a 24-hour race all the top name brands as in Ferrari 360 N-GT, Mosler MT900R, Porsche 996 GT3-RS, Porsche 996 GT3 and at the end of the 24 hours the lone 427C Monaro won be an impressive 23 laps So Holden in their wisdom built a road going version to be sold in 2003 2004 with a limited built numbers of 50 price tag of over $200000 and with the impressive 23 lap win they made a prototype code named HRT427 standing for Holden Racing Team 427 as in the cubic inches of the motor now comes 2003 we enter 2 Holden Monaro's and with a few new top brands as well surely they could take out the Australians? We don't even build super cars, the top brands are as listed BMW M3 GTR, Ferrari 360 N-GT, Mosler MT900R, Porsche 996 GT3-RS, Porsche 996 GT3-

RC, Lamborghini Diablo GTR, and at the end of the race after 24 hours the Holden Monaro's number 05 and 427 respectively finished 12 laps ahead of Porsche 996 GT3 RC 13 laps ahead of Porsche 996 GT3 S Cup and a super car in its own right the Mosler MT900R 20 laps down then the Porsche 996 GT3 Cup 32 laps down then the Porsche 996 GT3-RS 36 laps down then the Lamborghini Diablo GTR 40 laps down then the Porsche 996 GT3-RS 247 laps down then Porsche 996 GT3-RS DNF Porsche 996 GT3-RS DNF Ferrari 360 N-GT DNF then BMW M3 GTR DNF, late 2003 to 2004 it was canceled, now how I see it this stunning road car the mighty HRT427 never made into production it was just too good and two years running wins 2002 and come one two in 2003 24 hours and the only good thing that came out of it was Peter Brocks 10th Bathurst win all in our own Holden built and designed car right here in Australia,

I have some sad news as well I hear that even though Holden stopped making cars in Australia at the end of 2017 I hear that they have to now close all Holden dealerships by the end of 2021 and to make things worse, GM in America is going to bring down the Chevy and give us what we asked for before, when Holden stopped the V8 stopped rear-wheel-drive stopped manual's so only auto's available, let's see if GM takes away our Utes lets also see if they are going to try and call our beloved Utes as Trucks? I think if they do this they will fall with the same fate as Holden because we are a proud nation and our Utes are a huge part of our history almost as long as the auto industry here in Australia, Please GM I ask with all my heart to follow these ideas and you will prosper and I say this because Holden our car let us down and you can't just come to Downunder sell your biggest sellers like the Corvette and Camaro which are beautiful cars in their own right but we don't want that we want these things 1 our car! 2 Utes not trucks 3 SUV's or 4X4 are not trucks? 4 This one is very important With our racing heritage please remember with our most famous race here in Australia it is called Bathurst 1000 now you can race they're but not in the fashion of that race Holden V's Ford if you desire to take on the mountain we only have one King his name is Peter Brock 10 Bathurst's all in a Holden it has to be a whole new ball game a whole new race, not Camaro V's Ford because that would not be right, I and many others here in Australia have been very sad since the closure of our brand Holden when they stopped manufacturing and designing in late 2017 and when the ZB Holden Commodore came out for two years straight Holden had its worst sales on record so you can see we are very passionate about our car so like I said if you follow above you will be ok here try not to replace the Holden Icon brand with the bowtie Chevrolet we don't want that no matter how many of your top CEO's have said we can crack the Australian market because if you do it will fail.

Chapter 9 Tattoo's

Tattoos have been around for quite some time and when I was a young boy you only ever seen tattoos on a biker or a sailor and either one there was a meaning to them each tattoo had a story the sailor had the ship's anchor meaning ships were their whole life then you have bikers they would have sculls or flames something to do with their lifestyle you would have pin-ups their bikes even their partner's names or even some would have their bikers back patch would be on their arm partly to do with respect for their fellow member we are brothers the old saying blood in blood out,

No one else had tattoos back then and if did you would be seriously scorned for having a tattoo something to do with religion or it was just you must be a bad person but I knew when I grew up I would get tattoos and that was mainly because for a short time a had a member of the hells angels living behind my childhood house and I looked over the back fence and I see all these beautiful bikes and the head guy came out and called me over clearly because I was looking into his back yard now this guy was 6ft 4 built like a brick shit house he had long blonde hair and he showed me his bikes he was so nice to be nothing like how the town was painting him it was not long before they got thrown out because they were coming in late if night and the bikes were so loud but they never bothered me I found out some years later he got killed in some turf war it was sad because he was such a nice guy he was the leader of that chapter ill never forget him,

So I grew up and got several tattoos each one has meaning and now a lot of people have them just so they can get a few more Instagram likes, I mean come on why would you get a tattoo that is useless like I'm going to get a cactus and someone will say why are you getting that type of tattoo for and they will say o it looks cool not that it has a reference to when you were in the desert or anything,

My tattoos represent a broken heart from a failed marriage a deck of aces for my children overseas Ned Kelly's helmet because he stood for what he believed in then there is rose tattoo album cover then hells bells because AC/DC is my favorite band and also an ace of spades card on fire representing trying to clean my life from all the bad, at the time of writing this book I have six and one days soon I want more but whichever I decided to use I'm not sure which ones will be left out but I already have chosen quite a few I want two full sleeves and maybe a large back piece one day and when they say getting a tattoo you will want more is so true it is very addictive but I am old school and I like tattoos for their meaning, not something stupid just because it looks cool because they are the ones who in a few years will complain about their crap tattoo and want it covered not one of mine will ever be covered!,

Like I knew this person once who was a control freak she was supposed to be my friend well short story she wanted to marry me and I said no because she was not my type anyway and i was no where near ready so the next thing she does is gets a tattoo with mine and her name on her wrist in Arabic so no one would know what it said and of course as soon as she did not get the desired outcome she got it covered so no one knew what it meant to her so people moral of the story don't get a tattoo unless it has real meaning and if you are going to get your friends to name tattooed on you well you're a fool but if you must please have their permission to do so because tattoos are not cheap and a cover-up hurts,

I like tattoos that are black and gray or with lots of colour, i like them big or small and placement is a key and if you are a noob and have never had one dont ask will this hurt, yes their is mome pain involved but everyones pain level is diffrent like mine ive curently got five on my arms and non of the hurt but the two on my chest OMFG did that hurt it was the most pain ive ever felt in my life but other people get them there and they say they did niot feel it! maybe i just have a sensitve chest? Either way i love everone of my tattoos and im getting plentty more but for me the secret to having the best tattoos find a good tattoo artist its the only way you will get what you want and dont take what someone says do your reseruch.

Chapter 10 Truth And Lies

Truth or lies is a good rant I think because which side are you on the side of truth on any subject? at any cost? Or lies to suit you or to save yourself? I've been on the blunt end of lies things said that would rattle anyone's cage I've seen the truth which can just be as damaging when you see the reality! There is truth or lies in relationships in religion in nearly everything you can think about it just comes down to the % of protecting one's interests or your business or country's interest, you can lie about having an affair or lie about if there is a god or even aliens we all know the fallout, Is there a good time to lie? Should you always tell the truth? Lie or truth is up to you but no matter you can't say it's my fault when you speak your words, sometimes truthful words can cut you just as deep as a lie depending on the circumstances, Let's say for argument sakes that God is a lie now would this be a good thing to lie about? could you imagine if the truth finally came out how much would the world change I think it would end up in anarchy so if someone knew is that a good enough reason to keep telling a lie?

What about aliens let's say they are not real so why would they try and cover it up, So what the flying disc is now a weather balloon made of very weak wood so it's ok to lie about their not real because they're not? So why makeup all these cover stories and just say it was a weather balloon to start with? I don't think the government would be worried if someone got photos of such a balloon there is not a lot of technology in them and why roll out the army just for a balloon? It's like that saying burn your bridges you'll be better off so you burn the bridges and you can't stop thinking about that person tell me what that means sounds like a cocking bullshit to me, Now I get why you lied about sleeping around you were trying to save yourself because that was easier than telling me the truth and the truth is you loved us both so you let me go because that was the easier wasn't it? Truth and lies it's all in how you view the word wrong or right truth or lies that you tell is pretty much based on your humanity if you have any.

Chapter 11 Moods And Family

Why do I have to put up with your mood? If you have cracked the shits for whatever reason it does not give you the right to be nasty to someone else no wonder the world is such a fucked up place to be in, In this fast-paced life that we live no one can smile at anyone, it has to look like that they are so angry at the world so pissed at you for not looking at where you are walking that you say sorry for bumping into them all they can do is look at you and say whatever dickhead and you think to your self that you did say sorry what the hell was up to his ass? It's not to say that no one ever gets in a mood we all do but I think to attack other people because you're in a mood is not a God-given right to abuse another person just because you're in a little childish mood you know the ones like 6-year-olds have,

It is disappointing that you are so self-centered that all you seem to worry about is what's in your little world I mean take for instance that guy that bumped into before and you had a go at him? Do you know what he is going through in his life? Do you release the stress that you now have to put on him under? So how about you watch where you are walking instead because If you were on the ball you would be able to move out of his way saving him unneeded stress but know you think you are all that and then some that's why it washes off your back like it was the type of a blessing because you don't have to give it another thought now it's clear to me how much of a pig you are! So just remember people, the way you treat people is only what you are going to get back 10 fold so pay it forward smile and stop being a total asshole, Does it make you feel all-powerful that you can be a bully just tossing your weight around at will because it makes you feel like you are in control of everything well let tell you your ass is not worth a penny or dime.

family

How many in your family? Do you have brothers? Do you have sisters? Do you have both? Are you an only child? Do you have a family that is not blood? Family is not just a blood connection there is a family which are good friends and that also has an unbreakable bond are you lucky like me? How complicated is your family I have 3 brothers and one sister one of my brothers is two the same mother and father another brother who is from the same mother different farther one sister is to the same father different mother and the other brother has the same father but the same mother as my sister's mother, I have two dear friends that are family both mean a lot to me, we have a strong unbreakable bond just like my brothers and sister, how many in your family tree my family means the world to me what does it mean to you? Are you unbreakable? or do you just come and go with the damn breaze not having to many concernce if your family if worth fighting for even if it is just a dream? Some family come and go so care and some just don't? Others will have your back when your in trouble while the others wont care if you fall down the flight of stirs only a few are lucky to have someone in their family that sticks by you no matter the fault others will just wax and wayne with the seasons only coming around when they see something for offer, Family can be a blessing in discise some family will watch you choke no matter whats happening around them some family will love you uncondisionly other family will stay in contack all the time other familys it seems like forever since you last spoke! some familys love to spend money on their loved ones no matter if they are rich other familys will treat you like a homeless man so they dont have guilt when they dont get you anything! Dont get me wrong family is very imporntent but not all of us have a good one, Some familys fight all the time but somehow they seem to have this strange respect for each other! Some people would be shocked if they knew how other family members are treated and some if they knew might not even do anything about it! Family is not just your perants and theirs its you and your partner and children if there is any its not just your brothers and sisters as well its your pet dog or cat or what other pet you may have! but no matter the family that you have everone needs one

Chapter 12 Being Yourself And Animals

You being yourself sometimes is not that easy when you are judged purely on what shop you buy your clothes from people don't want to know you unless you have the latest phone the most expensive cars and huge houses with a swimming pool and butlers dysiner clothes fake friends on the right side of hollywood a high paying job like a lawyer dr or pollitition,

Why are people worried if you are wearing a t-shirt with a saying? I remember making my te-shirt saying and it was super dag and yes I put it on with pride and I did not care what anyone thought and that's something that has not changed it's the same with my music I don't care if you hate it or love it it's what I like and that's what matters to me or even on a te-shirt a favorite band you get scorned on and it used to be the same for tattoos now more people have them than not but when I was growing up you only had tattoos if you were a sailor or a biker now even the yuppies name them but they don't have any meaning to them it's all for the show to say look at me I'm wild when they are still just yuppies,

It's the same with cars you either a Holden man or a Ford man either red or blue and yes I am a Holden man up until the end of 2017 when they closed their doors here for building and disgnins our car and yes I own a Holden car and I love it and I truly don't give to flying pigs asses if you like my car or you don't that does not bother me at all it has my touch it has my feel to it but I too have been judged for because it did not suite some yuppie fuck because it did not have a BMW badge on the bonnet,

Please, people, don't follow what someones are doing have your mind and enjoy what you enjoy because life is very short not to live in a place where you are happy and drive the fucker don't let it just waste away in the shed or garage start it and take it for a drive! no point leaving it for someone else to wreck it or sell it after your dead.

animals

Some of us have dogs and some have cats some have both and some hate dogs or cats or both, what is your favorite animal? Mine would be an African Elephant, why did you pick that animal? I picked the African Elephant for many reasons I love they gracefulness I also love how they protect the young and they have a strong sense of family if you have ever seen an Elephant come across bones of an Elephant how it strokes the bones like the Elephant is sad and it stands still like it is giving a sign of respect maybe even grieving the loss of a family member? Plus I might add they look magnificent they are massive and have a strong bond as a group,

I don't like seeing them at the circus parading then like they are some sort of toy they need to be free I seen one documentary on tv and it was an Elephant that went rogue at a circus and they fired a shit load of bullets into the poor Elephant that maybe was sick of being chained up maybe a good idea I think just leave it in its natural surroundings o but we are humans we dont do that?,

It's not to say I hate the circus I don't at all I love watching the clowns being chased and the magic shows and sideshow alley but the part I hate is seeing these poor animals in captivity is just wrong people need to put them self's as the animals and the animals as the humans and I'm pretty sure by the end of the day all the Elephants would be returned to the wild and for the ones that would not survive than those get to go to a special farm just for Elephants where they can roam free and not in cages,

This is wrong what we do thinking we are all King shit and all that we need to leave alone these very beautiful animals and to those pouches, you should be captured and put in in chains then put in a cage and because we pouched him we can pull his teeth out one by one with nothing for the pain and leave him in that cage without freshwater or food and if he is lucky we will beat him to almost dead just to make him do tricks for all the Elephants in their seats, now would that not be different and you can bet your sweet ass that it would not be a day and many things would change,

We are just lucky that Elephants can't talk and hold a conversation we definitely would be fucked but then it would have never happened?

Have you seen an Elephant in the mud? They have so much fun like little kids how could you chain up such a beautiful animal? Is it all just for money, fame? What is it? I know a lot of them now are born into captivity but that does not mean you can't stop this now we are losing such graceful animals in the wild and it won't be too long before there will be no Elephants in the wild and the only way you will see them is either a zoo or the Internet or DVD, so come on people stop this madness and stop cutting off their tusk's you are nothing but cruel pouches all for money and greed well I hope someone hunts you down and cuts off your ball sack and leave your balls blowing in the breeze, you are lowlife scum bags, I doubt it if any of you even have s soul doing the things you do it's disrespectful and downright wrong and all the governments in the free world need to step in and save these beautiful animals before there are none left in the wild, give them a fair warning with what's going to happen then hunt down the poachers and put them through the court system and let the law deal with them.

Chapter13 Racist

Some white and some black people men women and children want devison all to do with getting money out of past events these people no matter of colour want to change names of things that have been since i was a child even before my mytime, I may even mention things that either side has come up with lets look at say white bread? now is white bread racist? no i dont think so what about toilet paper it is white but it is not sold as white toilet paper what about the roads we drive on are that not called black tar? or bitchiment? what about a white shirt or a black shirt is this not what they are so how are we now going to by a shirt that has nothing to do with race? am i not alowed to ware a white shrit or a balck shirt? i cant have brades in my hair? are you for real? this is going to far and i beleive that freedom of speach has a lot to do with it, both black or white people want peace? am i worng? if you want peace why try and stir the pot and if you dont want peace then go to a county who are fighting and pick a side maybe they are fighting the colour that you dont like with your white or black privlige, Im sick of every time i want to relax and watch some videos on the net and you have both mind you black and white woman abusing men because there where poilte and said hi i am trully like what the actual fuck or you have people pulling over cars of the oppsit colour and taking it out on them for things that happened to there great great great grandfather, Yes we had slaves yes it was wrong yes my culture took away babys from their mothers and gave them to white faimlys so am i supposed to now hate white people? no i dont hate white people but here is the kicker people are you ready I DONT HATE BLACK PEOPLE! so what is the go with that? I seen and heard stories at diffrent times and places where it was the whites chasing down the blacks and belted the hell out of the white guys then there was another time and it was another place it was black men chasing down white guys to beat the hell out of them! it is time for all of this bullshit to stop,

Was there not a time in the past that each of our race and this is before slavery! a time where diffrent humans wipped out diffrent speices of humans and some of the of other speices even interbread? like really? yes and they did this with no hate but some how as white man came from places and black men would somehow meet in times beofore and these times are not brought to our itention but somehow thw stupid whites tookm some black people and made them slaves and this is called white privlidge? NO sorry fuck you i am white and in my history we did not own slaves so how am i white privleage? please explane? I think to be truthful we are all guilty of some sort of racisim and if you trully beleive in your heart that im am white privlage then you are being racist but let me also tell you that i dont think that you are black and i dont say black lives matter because to say that is racist when all lives matter! the goverments all make the same mistakes lets let this silly people fight because there is more than balck and white and its noit that i was not sikened to more core as a human not of any colour or releigon or creed just a human i was sickened to see George Floud killed by the police and to me it would not matter if the cops where of colour and just the same if it was a white man on the ground and the cops are of colour to me it is the same and we need to stop with the BLM movment because it is racist and if you dont think that is racist then there is something wrong with the way you think? do you as a man or womanj of colour or white what do you think of Hittler? you both should have the same thought and that is? you are racist if you think Hittler was coolo Hittler was white but he killed whites o thats right they where killed becuase they where jews! was not Jeuse not white? so your saying to me that yes Jeuse was white but he is not white privlage because this is 2000 years ago? what time frame did we become white mprivlaged? o could that be like the 1600 1700 1800's this if any time in history is white privlage not to day and if today is included then you have to look at the rich and big corparations at white privlage?m its time to direct your angr to where it belongs and not at the poor white black or what ever fucking clolour you are so come on people its time to really look at the bigger puicture? its either you look at doing it right! as in taking it to the goverment in your country and hit them with the white privlage? or you just drop it all togerher because you would get any suport from all black people,

Question where does the white privlage start? how much black do you have to have in you to no longer be soon as white privlage? what is 50% black ok if so how can you tell a white mans true heratge bassed on you just looking at him if you looked at me you would not know i had black in me! but ive seen black people say to me o you are so privlages you white people so what is up with that? I trully believe if you want any whites or even half whites to start to listen to you you need to come up with a better answer then my great great great great ganddaddy was a slave? now if this is your only defence? you have toy relise that this was hundrends of years ago so lets look at enother thing to help sort out black and white stupidy my mother killed my step father my mother went to jail i had no where to go but a nice lady took me in and i was held for 20 years so what is my privlage? now you would not know that by lookinmg at me but because of my skin colour i am white privlage so see your black movment wont go any ferther than being racist instead of getitng behind your movment with facts relating to this day other wise it just looks like a money grab and anyway of always said if you trully beleive in this white privlage then go back to the bush or desert which eevery it is that you come from and live with noi power that white privlage gives you give up your phone which white privlage gives you give up your job and your money that white privlage gives you and all this does is gets you mad because somehow your not going to be happy till you have whites in slavery for a few hundred years now digest all thaqt and come out with somethng a little more pressing then you are white privlage,

Thousands of years in the harsh coditions little clothes hence the colour of your skin which if being tecical its not actualy black its like a dark brown but we dont call them brown people why is that? white skin less sun more clothed hence whiter skin broblem here also white people are not actualy white its more of a cream than white so what is the go here? now i know a lot of race wars have to do with slaves taken from their country people and sold into slavery and this is sad indeed then you come to a place like australia and youll see its the same but diffrent the men and women of colour first where slautered then white people stole their children and gave them to white familys because the white people beleived they will give those children a better life then you have the indans again white people took over their country and killed a lot of them made a lot of the men slaves and the women used for white mans plesure, yes the men and women of colour fought back a lot of them lost their lives a lot of children where now born from white and colour sexual incounters and in all of the voilince and all of the race wars that have been fought over thousands of years we are now not just a multiy coltural country we are a multiy world take me for excample how i think it is diffrent than most but that does not mean that i am wrong, I see the world not through rose coloured glasses but how it actualy is, Yes white black brindle yellow red and brown and in each of the colours their is a line that some will cross some wont and that has nothing to do with their colour religon or creed its just what you are inside, there is notning wrong with wanting to teach your children were you come from and to teach them some of the old ways but the ways we have to stop teaching our children is about war between white and black and to stop teaching the hateread that some people of any colour teaches their children, I myself in my hostory come from a line of colour but i am white so how could this be? let me tell you a short story that will show that colour of any sort only means something when it is full of happiness not full of either past events of future events as long as happness in the true sence, many moons ago a grandmother that i would never meet because it was genarations before i was born, a white man fell in love with a woman of colour full blood of her country she also fell in love with the white man they where happy and married with children, among both colours of people that their story had nothing to do with the coloured people who decided to try and take her children away from her because she had married a white man and the children where going to be raised by a white man, did the men of colour take into account she loved her husband? and did the white men and women of that town have the right to make her husband feel like he was a man with leprisy? the both side are in the wrong and that is a true story so tell me who had the right to try and destroy their happniess? yes it has been hundred of years but what has changed? the only thing that has changed is some people can see through the white and black problem! then there is white blet or black belt in karate is that not racist to white men or women? becauce the black blet is a sign of a higher rank? black then is stronger then white? no its just a colour? The problem is we are just to used to hating then loving and you may ask of what colour am i? in my DNA there is both white DNA and Black DNA so am i white or black? and what are my viues on black and white? well i am white! now i am I a white thinker or a black thinker? to be honest if i was to pick either I whould just be a hipocrit Ive looked at both sides of the history of colour vs not colour and it is both colours that have made the diffrence in the world yes some bad on some parts and some good at some points, We all must band together brown red yellow black and white to be one race of humans like we began as thousands of years ok and stop with this repration of wanting money for past genarations mistakes just to make you feel better when all it does is couses divisoins between cultures when we should all inbrace before we lose more of all coltures and that is what is sad, Ive watched Roots and if you havent i recomend that you do but what i took from watching the whole thing was we all all slaves no matter the colour because when you stick with i am white or i am balck i must destroy all others that dont share my idolige, love share it pass it on and dont be part of the problem be apart of the solotion! its starts with you now what are you going to do? and no it does not start with me because i already follow that rule so what are you gonna do brother?.

Im going to vent in this rant with all the bullshit that ive been going through latley while working hard on writing these chapters for my books which after my first book "Escaping a past" I deceided to write 4 books at once whitch to me they are very inportent and with this book "Old man rants" i wanted to put my point of uive out there as i have found my life my voice has been hidden over shadowed by my past and by my weakness to break free of the shackelss that have kept me in this never ending loop of crazyness and shame, yes i am pissed off with a lot of people and the constant onslout of acusatuions lies and scams all i have ever wanted is to be free, I have never felt truly free i feel like the past is just behind me waiting to spring out ant any moment ready to reclaim what is not theirs all beacuse i refuse to lay down like a dog thats been beaten almost to death I am tired and sick to my guts for trying, Ive pushed so hard to write these books no body knows what it is like to see things that are not there tired of hearing the voice's in my head I want out I want freedom I just dont want freedom as in being free i want all this black white racial tention to stop,

We as a human race are all tied to each other somewhere through our DNA but we act like if im white im priveliged if im black im perciquted because i dont burn in the sun, what is hard for me is being both black and white so what side do i take am I more black? or more white? would you care for me diffrent if i could change the colour of my skin? am I not more human than either white or black? so what is more important here being of coloured skin? or being human that cares for both colour no matter the religon or what side of the getoe you live on,

If all of you who read this trully think outside of the box for one secound would you reather be known as the man or woman that helped someone out or do you need to be known as the black man or woman or the white man or woman that helped someone out? to me there is way to much hateread between both races and you know there are more than white or black? and somehow you believe in a God that you cant see you have blind faith but what you dont see is the white or black man or woman beside you, There is nothing wrong with your culture there is nothing wrong with handing it down to the young and yes in genral whites do get the first pick in a work place lets say the boss who is hiring he would most likely pick a whiter man or woman or a black man or woman now revrse this and say a black man or woman is going for a job and the boss that is hiring see's black and whites standing outside the boss will most likely pick a black man or a black woman over a white person i thnik this is so wrong of any race to do that then you have all the other countrys that have there natives, I think the whole human race are like sheep you really only have a few that stand out from the crowd and these people should be reconisesed for their push to make people relise that we are all one just take Tom MacDonald for example the way he dresses it turns a lot of people off for some it might be the tattoos on his face or it most defintely would be the lyrics if you actuly listen to them? and this one man is breaking all the trends and all of the stigma that srounds rap that also surounds the stigma behind race colour creed within saying that he manages to stay true to himslef he dose not go mainstream he still stays underground, for me he sends a clear message 1 stop controling black and white culture 2 stop trying to tame down anyones words because i believe someone like him would be good runing a country and you might say why is that? i can tell you why! because you would know why you voted for him you would know there is no lies there is no twisting his words to mean something other that what it is meant to be no this is not a plug for his music i want people to truly be free like him true to express your true self, I also picked Tom MacDonald after i listened to his music I was hooked but i was not hooked just because he had sweat beats i did not just pick him because he dressed to be himself not to impress i also did not just pick him because his lyrics hit home for me but i then went to look at his back round and it was very aparent that his lyrics are not some copy cat rapper no not at all it is true life real pain and suffering like me and thats when i trully loved his music even more i conected with his music on such a deeper level than before and in all of the caouse and mehame i seen a man that loves his family and i trully beleive if anyone has had some kind of a life struggle you will get his music lets hope that anyone who trys to listens to his music that has never before but they are going to cheek it out for themselfs for the first time if you are not hooked by the mans beats lyrics or style then you ethier have not lived or you just have poor taste in music, MY genaration most dont listen to anyone like that but im not just a person who listens to what everyone else is listening to for me its also been fuck you both fingers in the air like stone cold steve aston all i can say out of all the diffrent msic that i listen to i trully hope that he makes it to the top which i dont even doubt it for a secound,

I went a little of side track there but thats on everything i write is writen to eithger pay homage to that person or to tare strips off of them, There are more than just a few people that need a puntch in the face and there are some i wont even mention them and yes i am sick and tired of living in shame all because my mother tried to protect me from the evil step father but that was instint the only time she showed it for love i dont think she knows what that is, My older brother shits me to tears he wont exnolage that i was beaten by her because to admit it is living in the past? are you for real bro? you did things to me that you wont admit to you keep telling me that you wish we where closer and i tell you i need to hear from you the truth so i know you would have my back, You keep putting her on a pedistal she was the best mother ever and you know that is a damn lie and that sadens me then he tells me to let go of the past because my past over shadows his loving past from our mother he tries to tell me that we all where naughty and that i was just a little more naughty and he remebrs the flogings and im like no way brother she never even laid a hand on you does he not get that i was there i remeber i was the only one screaming he can say yes i want you to move on so i dont shit on his memories but i find that hard to do when there is no exceptans from his side like egnolage what i have been through no he would reather live in a fucking bubble than be my brother standing by myside i just spoke with him the other day and we where talking about stuff and i found him not to be telling the truth so i called him out on his bullshit i told him that when mum went to jail i was left to fend for myself and this is true well no he tells me that it was me that took off then he kept saying i was this and i did that and im like na fuck off bro you have lost the plot then i told him to take the two dicks that he had in his mouth out because i think its pushing on his brain and its fucking with his memory i also told him i did not care if he showed everyone because i meant what i said,

By now now you would have figured that i can talk alot well i dont know if i can talk a lot but i have pleanty to write about and that i have! yes my mind wonders off and on point and sometimes i think of that boy i saved drowning i wonder if he would remeber me? I wonder to about that man that was blind drunk sititng in his car on the side of the highway he had a flat battry and we also most got whiped out by some maniac who was speeding with no headlights on and he almost colected us on the side of the road i keep going back in my mind about the time i came back from overseas and because i was so stressed and suffering PTSD i drove through two stops signs i keep thinking to myself how lucky i am to be alive and if another car was coming could of i missed it and i doubt that i would of i was sick and stressed i could not think straight i dint not give two flying fucks if i lived or died and to look back on that time i know i was crying for help i was screaming for help but no one could hear me not even myself with the amount of whisky that i was drinking i should be dead by now but a broken heart could not heal while sobar so staying drunk and not giving a fuck helped me to deal with it at the time yes i still get sick from it and the pills dont even work ive been in so much pain the best pain meds dont work glad in away though because i think i could of esaily thrown away the bottle back then just for something that would releive the pain but no that would be to easy, nothing works and we are in 2020 the time of tecolagie and advencmetns in medical seinace still i cant be pain free,

I guess this rant has moved all over the place and thats ok ive still got so much more to say I feel like i have let my children down when i came back from overseas why might you ask? i made a promise that i was coming back yes i know i thought i was and they are older enough now to know the truth and that is true but it does not stop my mind from wondering around and hurting, Yes the past has some horrble memories in it but in the present if is much brighter but i cant help but feeling like i have let people down yes i own all my parts of whats gone wrong in my life but i also wont take it up the rear just to gain some money or fame no thats not me i wont sell out i wont pretend to save myself i have always gone against the grain if it dont sound right then dont trust it, Ive always said if i ever have money I would always look after my crew and that i always will do there is something that is more powerful than onces self, Yes i have tattoos and if you dont like that then go nick yourself I dont need your negitivety in my life thats one reason why I escaped in the middle of my life i needed to do it my way with no drama plus there was a price on my head at one stage but it was more a price on my head if the old house mate could find me and do you know that not one day has gone by where im still not looking over my shoulder waiting for it to show its ugy head again and i can tell you she might not like what she sees anymore im no longer the timad young boy anymore I grown ive lived and ive even done things that you would of loved to of done but you want to keep living in your bubble just like my brother you to would make a good pair i mean come on bro you team up with her so you could steal my stuff all while you where a big ass christine now you tell me that you dont beleive in god? man you need to check yourself before you wreck yourself! Just like that time you stole my papper run money that i had been saving for a BMX bike and you flately said no it was not me and the only other person in the house was our mother but your answer instead of saying yeah sorry bro you said well it was not me and it was not mum you must of misplaced it? i still have never got the truth out either of you so which one was it? yes as ususal no answer?

Im actully sitting out in the sun in an alyway while writing this chapter watching all the busses going past and the airoplanes above I can hear the birds cherping there is a soft brezze blowing and this whole time ive not once thought about Covid19 and you know i should be very worried about it but im not ive been caged up for six months and its so nice to smell the fresh air, how many of you apresate your life? well let me tell you the grass is not greener it is only like that if you live with someone or are housemates with someone who is a complet control freak then by far it is defiantly greener on the otherside but if you are a play around then no it is not greener it is just diffrent but not greener as long as your not in a toxic friendship or relashionship anything is better than living like that, I do however have to say this i get it now I get you either have to take it in the ass to make it or you basically sit on a shelf wasting your talent and only a few that dont take it in the rear are strong enough to make it even in doing so it could kill them, I wonder if any of you who have got to this point of my book and say man I love this guy I wish i could be like him! and you know you can first you have to always stay true to who you are! 2 you have to stop blaming yourself and start giving less fucks if people like you 3 live your life your way if it makes you happy then do it as long as its not going hurt or kill someone 4 be free in mind body and spirt 5 if you are a beleiver in God it does not bother me but remeber dont force your beleif's onto other people 6 love yourself you might be the only person that does 7 if this fits you then stop being such a control freak 8 get out of the city once in awhile to recharge yourself 9 dont be judgemental on any subjet because you are not perfect so dont judge 10 stay happy,

If you dont beleive in white privlige what about a black man who says he is white what about that same black man he dont just beleive he is white he takes mesdince to change the pigment in his skin now why would you do that? this man is famous his name is micheal Jackson so is his black life that matters now turned white matter? the problem now you have white men white women doing the same as Jackson and if you now look at them they may have dark skin but the look nothing like a natural born dark person, there is to much bullshit going on and im not being rude or selfish it is these people who are making the world crazy but before i go in to what is crazy let me state that i am not for black or white im not homeafobic i dont have nothing against bie drag ladyboy i have no problem with you wanting to make your face look like a barbie its your body your choise i dont even have any feelings to judge if aliens landed and they all looked like they were from starwars and yes i do hate a few people and ill state them here Mum, Dad, Besite and WF the rest of the world i dont judge so dont judge me and dont judge anyone else now comes the crazy part I'm asking for you not to judge me im only speaking the truth here it goes, black white brindle yellow red and that and this is only a few of the names its pretty bad, Nigga, Aethiopian Negro, or Black","Wigga, Caucasian or White"," Slanty eyes, Slap Head, Gooks, Mongolian or Yellow","Native American, American or Red" and "Malayan or Brown" Aboriginal, Native Australian, Abo, Gronk, Now im born of both black and white but i am neither my mother always told me that i am black now i tottally disagree with that statement i am not black nor white nor Native Australian nor Abo not even a Gronk what i am though is straight up human yes i love my country but i dont love the division that the stigma of being black lives matter or white privliage so i say to you who is reading this book dont fall for the rasict propaganda you are human and the sooner you relilse that then you can join me in being human on our one planet that we share its time to stop with whites took most conturys blacks become slaves jwues murdered in the millions the bomb was droped twice and killed many peral harbour destroyed while treaty was being signed but thats not the worst and i can tell you who mis the worst out of every race are you ready?

All of us the only ones that are not racist or bigets are the ones that are still native to their contury and live the old ways without tecnoligy even without petrol drivien cars the ones who don't use power to have light or to cook and these people are the ones that live without hate, with these people they live life their is no judgment because everyone wares the same clothes same everything and yes they might burn fires and they might kill animails to servive then you have us the white privelage black haters or the black Nigga slaves what about Slapheads Mongolian or those Abo's Native Australians and all of these people are what? bigots fanatic rasicts prejudice chauvinists xenophobia homophobe dogmatizer extremist partisan modern feminists haters and the list goes on and on, I am trully sick of all of this race war and now all you whites and all you blacks and all the other colour and named words of being racsit so lets turn it around lets make all the walls in all the houses around the world black and say all the roads around the world lets make them white and lets make all the light globes in every house black and why not make all the black cars aross the globe white now lets be even more prosice make all the airoplanes in the world black and and lets make all the jack daniles bottles white why not make all the white goods black stove or oven and fridge, microvave oven, washing michne and dryer now is not the world a better place but we can do more though to help out this war of colour, lets change all the light switches black and lets make all the tiolets black why not change the carpet in every house to white and i think all the this just makes my heart feel so much better what are you guys smoking there was no intention when a colour is made if you trully think with your mind why do you think we dont have black walls in a house? if you really have to ask that question then there probley is no chance that you will understand its also another reason why we are in this mess.

Chapter 14 Last Rant

Truth or lies is a good rant I think because which side are you on the side of truth on any subject? at any cost? Or lies to suit you or to save yourself? I've been on the blunt end of lies things said that would rattle anyone's cage I've seen the truth which can just be as damaging when you see the reality! There is truth or lies in relationships in religion in nearly everything you can think about it just comes down to the % of protecting one's interests or your business or country's interest, you can lie about having an affair or lie about if there is a god or even aliens we all know the fallout, Is there a good time to lie? Should you always tell the truth? Lie or truth is up to you but no matter you can't say it's my fault when you speak your words, sometimes truthful words can cut you just as deep as a lie depending on the circumstances, Let's say for argument sakes that God is a lie now would this be a good thing to lie about? could you imagine if the truth finally came out how much would the world change I think it would end up in anarchy so if someone knew is that a good enough reason to keep telling a lie?

What about aliens let's say they are not real so why would they try and cover it up, So what the flying disc is now a weather balloon made of very weak wood so it's ok to lie about their not real because they're not? So why makeup all these cover stories and just say it was a weather balloon to start with? I don't think the government would be worried if someone got photos of such a balloon there is not a lot of technology in them and why roll out the army just for a balloon? It's like that saying burn your bridges you'll be better off so you burn the bridges and you can't stop thinking about that person tell me what that means sounds like a cocking bullshit to me, Now I get why you lied about sleeping around you were trying to save yourself because that was easier than telling me the truth and the truth is you loved us both so you let me go because that was the easier wasn't it? Truth and lies it's all in how you view the word wrong or right truth or lies that you tell is pretty much based on your humanity if you have any.

We start of this rant about UFO's and the possible chance that we are not alone in the universe, when you think of a UFO you think little green men from mars, now for a start personally I think that if we are not alone then we have a higher chance of these creatures being more like star wars than little green men but anything is possible, Take a look back in time now to the very late 1800s were I might add a UFO crashed and the occupant died from their injuries now the conspiracy part of this problem is it was not until the early 1900's that we had a flight with the right brothers a not very flight worthy of great height's or distance so what crashed the crash? So, either we have a real spaceship that crashed, or we had humans first flight way before the 1900's so which one is it?

Then we move to a much later time 1947 to be precise were a UFO had crashed in the desert now as the story goes their where at least 4 body's approximately 4ft tall 3 of them died due to their injuries but one lived and was walking around true or not true? So you have many people that arrive and they see what was described as a disc-shaped object badly damaged now the military turn up and take over but the strange thing is they tell the reporters that it was a flying disc that crashed now why would the military say that when one it was just a weather balloon even if it was extremely important to keep it a secret and I am pretty sure most people could tell what looked like a disc-shaped object, so why tell the UFO story to the press if the only latter to say about their top secrets weather balloon so which one is it UFO or weather balloon? You decide,

For me it comes down to no matter if it is real or not you just have to look at the facts ok let's say that every UFO sighting is a top military project why would they land on in a school ground in Australia where it was seen by hundreds of people that's a bit silly don't you think? Or the big one just recently a big triangle UFO why would you let this be seen by not just the surrounding people but for it to be picked up on TV for the next lot of new Stuff? Now I'm not saying that it is a stunt by aliens or humans to sway you to believe or not to believe in one or the other I'm saying this is what I see now it's up to you to say yes that makes sense or your just a wacko author of this book, This might be true but there are many cultures out there that have recorded strange lights in the sky some even date back 1000,00. thousand it's in artwork dating back way before a man could fly the first plane made by the right brothers in 1903 so how could there be any kind of craft flying around even 100 years before that or even a 1000 plus years how is this possible? when both facts are easy enough to get hold of so do your research and send me an email if you find damming proof that UFO's are not real so go do your research and I don't mean the first thing you read go deep and try and find the true you might be surprised.

I have seen strange lights in the sky now was it a secret military aircraft? Was it a UFO? I see in the night sky two balls of light they constantly stayed the same distance apart moving left to right up and down zig zagging all over the sky they were moving quite fast then they would slow down I'm looking at this thinking I wonder what it could be not saying it's one of the other than after a few minutes it just shot up and incredible speed there was no sound so what was it? You decide! It's always hard to say yes I seen this and that from one person's point of view when we all could be wrong and if this is all a hoax by the governments around the world why would they hoax I understand the backlash from religions all over the world and if that is the case why to let them be seen not just by one but thousands so you can see why I might be a little confused,

Then you have leaked video of a UFO built by the military looks like it can barely get off the ground so how did they get them up so high when it looked like it could not even fly? And if this was a hoax why would they go to the lengths to build one to leak the video out so we can believe that UFOs are real? That to me makes no sense whatsoever so what would be the point behind leaked photos of one nation trying to make one? Was it because maybe after recovering one they could not figure out the technology, so they wanted to build them self-one? I mean you could easily come up with 10 just as valid reasons is to why they made one the same as the crashed UFO 10 other reasons it's possible or covered up its just crazy, It's always hard to say yes I seen this and that from one person's point of view when we all could be wrong and if this is all a hoax by the governments around the world why would they hoax I understand the backlash from religions all over the world and if that is the case why to let them be seen not just by one but thousands so you can see why I might be a little confused,

Why is it so hard to believe that another species just as smart or even in space much smarter could exist? what area in the night sky could host such beings? Such life that is so far away they would have to know how to bend space and time at will and of course no one or nothing is smarter than humans as we are so backward in thinking like say the closest star is 20 light-years away it would take 20 light-years to get to earth and 20 light-years to get home that's 40 light-years in total so that would sound a little farfetched, we can only hope they can figure it out before I'm too old to witness it I want to know do they fly how fast can they travel and can we go faster the speed of light? If so, how much faster can they go? Do they have mother ships? How big are they? Can they travel at the speed of light? Is it like Star Wars? Teaming with all types of exotic plants and animals and if there is life in other words? we just have not found them that does not mean they are not real we are just too sheltered and also too stubborn to think outside the box before we can't turn back the clock and look after the earth it's the only home we have for now until we can learn how to start a new planet even if that means making a new home,

There is a theory out there that says we did not come from here and that is possible our early cells that would start over millions of years what ended up with is a rock that bounces off of another planet or even another rock and it lands here and seeds the life that we know call home so under that conclusion there would be another planet out there at least hosts life and no matter if I believe that earth is not the only planet to host any form of life and to think that we have the only planet that can host life shows our true arrogance on how cocky we think we are no wonder the aliens don't want to come here why would you want to come to a planet where most likely they would nuke you as soon as you land.

flat earth conspiracy this is one of the biggest and most stupid conspiracies of all time it's as bad as saying a UFO was a Weather balloon or Swamp gas or even a Radar reflector or you come up with the Moon landing was fake, The flat earth conspiracy is so far wicked I know it came in a time when we thought the stars where lights hanging like it was on the ceiling and I just wonder why that has not taken off like the flat earth has, I mean how crazy is it truly? look at it like this they don't doubt that all of the other planets are round and our moon and sun are also round so why is the Earth flat? I also saw one very good piece of fact? that points to the Earth is round and the flat earthers believe and I think because back when the map of the known world they believed it was flat and they also believed that they would full off the edge of the world but some very smart people came up with their theory upon doing their experiments and with each one said the world was a globe and the churches did not want to know because that was heresy, they had to keep their secret, who would know what would have happened but to me it is clear the world is a globe not a globe with the top half cut off, I think you would be hard pressed to find any person that has done their schooling to say that the earth is flat plus I can't even see why you would even believe it too began with, with all the videos I have watched and all the flat earthers have not even given me one fact that proves otherwise because we all say you need to back up what you're saying not with some lose beliefs that did not stand up then let alone now,

Another conspiracy is a story from the bible take Noha's big boat and how it rained for 40 days and 40 nights! the biggest problem I have with this one let me take you on a ride now close your eyes and listen to what I am saying, You have this boat that's made of just wood now he gets all the animals from the world the problem back then it was only the known world right? let's say that it was the whole world! so Noha take his family gets them to travel to all parts of the world and to get each animal a male and female know that would take so much time? and then you have the boat built all animals all aboard and then comes this biblical rain now do the math it rains so hard that the whole world floods now the highest peak on earth is Mount Everest at just over 29,000 ft, So let's take 29,000ft and the whole globe covered to at least 29,000ft this much water for one would as in rain would have flooded the boat but let's again say ok the earth was flooded to at least 29,000ft at this altitude there is little to no oxygen so most of the animals would have died also including the humans on the boat so I guess to say that you have little food a biblical down poor not a lot of oxygen they all would have died plus when the boat makes landfall some 40 place days later it would have crashed into some mountain killing any remaining animals and humans and also there would have not been any humans to great or that would have survived that amount of water so no humans no animals so how did they survive? take into again the rain the altitude no food no fresh water no oxygen and half the animals would of ate the ones that would of died before the lack of oxygen killed the rest also means killing all humans on board, and if you have ever seen a body of water that sits across the road and say its only 1 or 2 feet in depth now it sits there for days before we see it slowly go down so explain it to me how at the whole world is covered in water to at least 30,000ft after a 40 day and night down poor and it just disappears in a matter of moments because it would have to as there would not of been enough food for 40 days let alone the months it would of taken for the water to have gone down far enough for the boat to hit land now they say that they have found it in a country called Turkey and it is just about 3700ft at sea level now if the math says you need up to 30,000ft of water to cover the whole Earth and now after 40 days and nights and clearly now the water level has to hit at least down to 3000ft that's 27,000ft from sea level water covering the whole glob how long do you think it would take for the water to drop enough for it to hit land clearly it would have to be months if not years! so tell me, dear believers, how do you make me believe that the water dropped like undoing a plugin a bath makes me understand how you see that after knowing some real facts and after doing some reading they have worked out that they were on the ship for more than a year, so the bible has one big ass lie, you are the judge! then, of course, you have the Yeti, Loch Ness monster, Giant humans, Alien abduction, Top secret government black budgets, Flight 19, The Philadelphia experiment, Men in black, Area 51, That's just to name a few.

Intermission

Political wrongness, red tape, kickbacks, money talks, and bullshit walks, Learn, Learn a lesson or get caught in her web is she a black widow or a wicked witch? Better run before she sees you; you'll get caught up in her smile, the lies will just wash over you, how smart are you because you won't see it coming? You'll lose all direction and all control it will be hard to breath when your with her & even harder to let go once she has a hold of your heart you'll be forever stuck in the time of memories that keep you from moving on, You dropped the walls that kept you safe I did not see it coming I truly got caught up in the whirlwind romance, you got my head spinning like a spinning top I'm totally out of control you did this to me I can't see a way out, look what you've done to me.

A vortex of love

I'm stuck in a black hole I can't move forward I can't move back your love has me grounded in this super-hot mix of emotions, Your love is like a vortex swirling around in my head I can't stop thinking about you why am I not strong enough to make it stop your grasp is so powerful over me, A supernova happened in my heart because of you an explosion of colour and emotions happened to me I did not see it coming I was hit right in the heart blinded by your beauty and bright shining light,

There is no void between the feelings I have and the same feelings you won't admit too there's only loneliness now that you're gone, I wished to be back in your arms at the speed of light touching your soft skin just one more fucking time but that would not change anything between me and you, I feel like Mars all alone no one really to talk too or no one that understands enough to care,

How do you move forward when the gravity of my feelings keep my stuck in this one place of mind were can my feelings run to before they come flooding right back, The light that emanates from you drew me in and kept me grounded you are like the Sun drawing me in and keeping me there just where you want me I'm like Mercury totally under your control I'm hot and flustered because of the pull that you have on me.